REINSURANCE
UNDERWRITING

REINSURANCE UNDERWRITING

BY

ROBERT KILN

AND

STEPHEN KILN

SECOND EDITION

LONDON   NEW YORK   HONG KONG
1996

LLP Ltd.
Legal and Business Publishing Division
27 Swinton Street
London WC1X 9NW

USA AND CANADA
LLP Inc.
Suite 308, 611 Broadway
New York, NY 10012 USA

SOUTH EAST ASIA
LLP Asia Ltd.
Room 1101, Hollywood Centre
233 Hollywood Road
Hong Kong

© Robert Kiln and Stephen Kiln, 1996

First published 1989
Second edition 1996

British Library Cataloguing in Publication Data
A catalogue record for this book is available from the British Library

ISBN 1 85978 066 0

All rights reserved. No part of this publication may be reproduced, stored in a retrieval system, or transmitted, in any form or by any means, electronic, mechanical, photocopying, recording or otherwise, without the prior written permission of LLP Ltd.

Text set 10 on 12 pt Baskerville by
Mendip Communications Ltd.
Frome, Somerset
Printed in Great Britain by
WBC Print Ltd., Bridgend, Mid-Glamorgan

PREFACE

This is not intended as another reinsurance textbook for students; however, every serious student should have a copy as it will give an insight into the real world of reinsurance that he could not get from all the textbooks. It is written in the form of notes deliberately and does not necessarily pose correct solutions to problems but is designed to make the reader pose his own solutions to his own problems. It is intended as a practical workbook for those who are working in insurance or reinsurance and who have a working knowledge of the subject, and for those who own or manage reinsurance operations.

We assume that the reader has a basic knowledge of reinsurance and knows, for example, what a second surplus treaty is, and knows the difference between an ultimate net loss clause and a costs clause.

The idea of a workbook of this nature arose from a very pleasant visit Robert Kiln made to Bangkok in May 1982 to attend a seminar on "Underwriting Inwards Reinsurance Business", organised by Mr C. N. Shastri of Asia Reinsurance Corporation, who published the proceedings in a workbook form. We would like to acknowledge our debt to him, also to Jim Bannister and Insurance and Reinsurance Research Group. They suggested the idea, made many suggestions and typed the many examples in Chapters 6 and 7.

The workbook is set out in a way that we hope will interest the reader and allow him to follow a consistent story, which is that of:

THE UTOPIAN REINSURANCE COMPANY

"Utopia"—"An imaginary state" described by Sir Thomas More (one of Robert's and Stephen's ancestors) in his political romance or satire (*Utopia* AD 1516).

"Utopia—Any ideal state of perfection" (Chambers' Dictionary).

The object of this book is to contribute to the improvement of reinsurance underwriting. If it does that it will have been worthwhile. And if it does that, even in a small way, to your underwriting it will have been well worth your money.

April 1996   ROBERT KILN AND STEPHEN KILN

THE UTOPIAN REINSURANCE COMPANY

This is the story of a mythical reinsurance company set up by Robert Kiln in late 1982 with a paid up capital of US$10,000,000 as described in Chapters 1–5.

Chapter 6 sets out various examples of reinsurance propositions that were underwritten or rejected by Robert in 1982, 1983 and 1984, with some footnotes written by the authors in 1995 after reviewing his underwriting decisions with the benefit of hindsight!

As might be expected, the company prospered and in 1988 its capital and surplus were increased to US$40,000,000, and his son Stephen Kiln, who had joined him as deputy underwriter in 1985, took over as underwriter in 1990. Chapter 7 relates this growth and contains 1989 examples with Robert's comments and underwriting decisions. Again, footnotes written in 1995 are included.

Chapter 8 describes the company's growth up to 1995. By that time, Robert had retired and the underwriting had been fully taken over by his son Stephen Kiln. Chapter 8 shows the revised underwriting philosophy introduced by Stephen. Chapter 8 continues with some examples of the 1995 placings offered to Stephen and his underwriting analysis and decision on each one.

NB Although our company is mythical its results closely resemble actual experience. The period 1983–89 follows Robert's own results in the period 1968–74 and good reinsurers' results in London for 1983–89. Its 1989 to 1995 experience is closely based on the results of Stephen's underwriting in that period and mirrors his success. So the Utopian's results are based on actually obtained rather than fictional figures.

THE AUTHORS

ROBERT KILN, born in 1920, is the son of a distinguished marine underwriter, R. L. Kiln. He started work in Lloyd's in 1937 with the Bowring non-marine syndicate for which Matthew Drysdale was underwriter.

As a Territorial in the H.A.C. he was called up in August 1939 and was commissioned in the Hertfordshire Yeomanry. He took part in the D-day landings and was seriously wounded three months later near Antwerp, losing a leg and suffering permanent deafness.

Returning to Lloyd's in 1945 he rejoined the Drysdale syndicate to work on treaties and reinsurance. He was an innovative non-marine underwriter and was responsible for many new developments in non-marine reinsurance such as index-linked third party cover and the use of excess covers to replace pro-rata reinsurance. Many Kiln wordings, in such areas as catastrophe and stop-loss reinsurance, gained wide acceptance and he was a pioneer in the reinsurance of captive insurance companies.

In 1962 he formed his own underwriting agency and the Kiln 510 non-marine syndicate, remaining underwriter for 510 and 557 until 1974 when he handed over to Colin Murray. He remained Chairman of the Kiln agency until May 1985, presiding over its development into one of the largest Lloyd's agencies with seven syndicates.

Robert Kiln has played an active role in Lloyd's affairs, with nine years as a Member of the Committee of Lloyd's. For some years he was Member and Chairman of the Audit Committee and was responsible for many proposals that have helped to develop and strengthen the Lloyd's role. He was one of those largely responsible for the formation of Lloyd's Life and was a director under Sir Henry Mance and was its Chairman from 1979 until 1985.

He is well known for his cogent presentation of forthright views and has been very active in reinsurance education as a speaker and writer on all aspects of reinsurance. His book *Reinsurance in Practice* has become a classic and second and third editions have been published.

His contribution as an active amateur archaeologist has been recognised by his election as a Fellow of the Society of Antiquaries and he was honoured with a Doctorate of Letters (D Litt) by Sheffield University.

His book *D-Day to Arnhem with the Hertfordshire Gunners* was published in 1992 and reprinted in 1994. His latest book *Ware and Hertford From Birth to Middle Age* (with Clive Partridge) was published in 1995.

STEPHEN KILN, born in 1951, is the son of a distinguished Lloyd's non-marine underwriter and author.

He was educated at Haileybury College and Sheffield University, reading Biochemistry. After a brief period of biochemistry research he joined American Risk Management (Hopewell), a captive management company.

He first entered the London Market when he joined Terra Nova Insurance Company in 1980 as underwriting assistant and quickly began underwriting in his own mode. He left in 1988 to establish a treaty account for Le Rocher Re (Prudential Re). The company prospered under his management in a difficult market and grew from a premium of under £1,000,000 to nearly £40,000,000 in six difficult years.

He left Le Rocher in 1995 after a change of management direction and has now followed his father and grandfather into Lloyd's. He has now joined Syndicate 991 A. E. Grant & Others to build up the non-marine reinsurance account. His underwriting emphasis has always been to look at all classes and territories on their own merits. The diversity of the portfolio at Le Rocher enabled it to survive and prosper when others were failing.

He used to help his father on many archaeological excavations (digs) around Hertford. He now lives there with his wife and two children.

CONTENTS

Preface	v
The Utopian Reinsurance Company	vii
The Authors	ix

CHAPTER 1 1983: SETTING THE SCENE 1—LINE LIMITS AND RETENTIONS	1
Setting the scene and setting our net line limits	1
Summary: maximum net lines	8
Maximum percentage lines	9
CHAPTER 2 1983: SETTING THE SCENE 2—EXPENSES AND OTHER MATTERS	11
On excess of loss and stop loss reinsurances	13
Our outwards treaty programme	14
CHAPTER 3 1983: SETTING THE SCENE 3—ACCUMULATION AND REINSURANCE PROTECTION	17
Catastrophic protection, our general excess programme	17
Other general reinsurances	18
Third party reinsurance	18
Marine hull, cargo and oil rigs	18
Other reinsurances	19
Stop loss reinsurance	19
Accumulation exposures	20
Exposure controls	20
CHAPTER 4 1983: REINSURANCE SYSTEMS AND CONTROLS	23
(1) Underwriting data	23
(2) Accounts	23
(3) Claims	23
(4) Outwards reinsurances	24
(5) Recording liabilities for excess of loss and stop loss inwards business	24

(6) Underwriting statistics 25
Thoughts on computers 28

CHAPTER 5 1983: OTHER REINSURANCE UNDERWRITING PROBLEMS 31

A. Reserving 31
B. Currency 34
C. Investment of the premium fund and reserves 35
D. Cash flow control 35
E. Decision-taking 35
F. The team 36
G. Integrity 37
H. Constructive underwriting 39
I. Disputes 39

CHAPTER 6   UNDERWRITING EXAMPLES 1983–1985 41

Aides-memoire to underwriting assessment 42
Proposition 1 USA Fire 1st Surplus 45
Proposition 2 German Fire 1st Surplus 49
Proposition 3a Philippine Fire 1st Surplus 52
Proposition 3b Philippine Fire 2nd Surplus 53
Proposition 4 USA Fire Q.S. 56
Proposition 5 Lloyd's Q.S. Confiscation 60
Proposition 6 UK Coy Catastrophe 63
Proposition 7 USA Fire Risk Excess 70
Proposition 8 French Hail Stop Loss 74
Proposition 9 Japanese P.A. Treaty 76
Proposition 10 Japanese P.A. Excess 78
Proposition 11 Asian Motor Q.S. 80
Proposition 12a UK Motor Excess 84
Proposition 12b UK Motor Excess 85
Proposition 13 German Motor Damage Excess 88
Proposition 14 Australian T.P. Excess 90
Proposition 15 USA Casualty Excess 93
Proposition 16 USA Casualty Excess 100
Proposition 17 Eastern European Marine Excess 105
Proposition 18 African Marine Hull Surplus 108
Proposition 19 Japanese Marine Hull Surplus 111
Proposition 20 African Marine Excess 113

CHAPTER 7   UTOPIAN REINSURANCE 1983–1989: UNDERWRITING EXAMPLES 1988–1989 117

Analysis codes 118
Proposition 21a UK Coy Catastrophe 119
Proposition 21b UK Coy Catastrophe 120

Proposition 22 UK Fire Surplus	126
Proposition 23a USA Medical Per Person Excess	130
Proposition 23b USA Medical	131
Proposition 24 USA Catastrophe	133
Proposition 25 London Coy Catastrophe	141
Proposition 26 L.M.X. Excess	146
Proposition 27 L.M.X. Marine	150
Proposition 28 Australian Catastrophe	155
Proposition 29 Japanese Catastrophe	159
CHAPTER 8 UTOPIAN REINSURANCE 1989–1995	**163**
Our adjustments to underwriting 1989–1994	164
Plan for 1995	165
Proposition 30 USA Catastrophe	166
Proposition 31 Australian Catastrophe	173
Proposition 32 Japanese Catastrophe	178
Proposition 33 Oil Rig Q.S.	181
Proposition 34 UK Motor Excess	187
Proposition 35 Aviation Franchise	194
Proposition 36 London Risk Excess	197
A UTOPIAN POSTSCRIPT 1996–2010	203
Index	205

CHAPTER 1

1983: SETTING THE SCENE 1—LINE LIMITS AND RETENTIONS

SETTING THE SCENE AND SETTING OUR NET LINE LIMITS

Cast

You: providing capital and financial backing for a reinsurance operation and providing ongoing financial control and investment.
Me: the potential reinsurance underwriter.

Scene 1: To establish our motives

Why do you want to get into this business?
Why do I want to be an underwriter?

We are starting this way because it is absolutely vital at the outset for the two partners in a reinsurance underwriting operation to have absolute trust in each other and for both parties to establish the motives of the other and that those motives coincide.

Now you, as the owner, may wish to come into the business for a number of reasons. Let us take a few examples:

(a) You may be a government whose main concern is to establish a government reinsurance operation for prestige reasons or to conserve the country's foreign exchange.
(b) You may be a businessman who wishes to provide a source of funds for investment purposes.
(c) You may be an investor with plenty of unused capital looking to build a substantial business fairly quickly.
(d) You may be a conservative investor looking to establish a business that will grow gradually and which can finance itself out of the profits generated.

Or you may combine a number of these motives.
I may be:

(a) An ambitious person wanting to make my fortune as quickly as possible.
(b) Someone who relishes power and prestige.
(c) A conservative type who wants a gentle, quiet life.
(d) A person who likes the challenge but who wishes to build his career steadily.

I will probably combine these and other qualities. Successful enterprises will need a mix of controlled enterprise and caution.

Now for the purpose of this handbook. You are going to be a type (d) investor and you are looking for a type (d) underwriter. Our motives gel together. This is not to say that (a), (b) and (c) are wrong. Investors of types (b) and (c) will want an (a) or (b) type underwriter. It is no good their employing a (c) or (d) type underwriter as the underwriter will be under constant pressure to take on more business than he himself feels prudent and he will end up with an ulcer. There are many examples where investors and underwriters of like type have got together and developed a reinsurance operation very quickly; even whole markets have grown quickly.

To write, say, US$50,000,000 of volume in, say, three years in a worldwide operation has been achieved many times in the 1970s and 1980s. In all but a few cases it must mean that such a volume will sustain a substantial technical or underwriting loss, which may be offset by investment income. Cash flow underwriting premium on long-tail classes must mean that the eventual losses will be within the area of US$75,000,000 to, say, US$100,000,000 when settled, but, as the average length of settlement may be seven years, the operation, properly reserved and well invested, is not necessarily wrong. But we are going to leave that to more adventurous souls who like mistresses with fur coats and diamonds.

We both have spouses and children to bring up.

Scene 2: Objectives

To underwrite a worldwide (including USA) general reinsurance account.
To establish the operation slowly and to underwrite for an underwriting profit by year three.
To finance future growth of the company from the profits generated.
To work towards a premium income of US$25,000,000 for year five, but there is no objective to write any minimum volume for any year.

In a Lloyd's syndicate we will want enough Names to provide a premium income capacity of around £10,000,000 increasing, say, to £20,000,000 by year five.

In 1983 a capital of US$20,000,000 would be preferable and allow for greater freedom of underwriting and easier acceptance of our security by our clients. However, we are going to start with a paid-up capital of US$10,000,000.

Scene 3: Assumptions

I am not going to dwell on where our office will be set up, whether the account will be limited to brokers or will include direct client business, as this will depend on the location and nationality of you and me. Neither in this book am I going to dwell at great length on financial projections of expenses and investment income. These are, of course, of vital importance but there are many better qualified than myself to deal with them.

It is our purpose to design and operate an underwriting operation to achieve our objective with the financial means at our disposal. We are also going to underwrite almost every class of business from all over the world with the exception of life reinsurance.

This assumption is for the purposes of this book. In practice, and with a new company, we would be best advised to concentrate initially on the areas and types of business about which the underwriter, or underwriters, have an expertise. Having set the scene we can now start planning our actions and our methods.

Management

Before we discuss underwriting we should talk for a moment about team work, people and organisation, i.e. management. You, as the proprietor, will operate through a board of directors of which you are going to be the chairman. That board will have as executive directors, myself as the underwriter and chief executive, my senior deputy(ies), plus an investment director and an administrator. This will be our executive management team; this team will meet at least monthly.

They will set underwriting policy, e.g. major types of business, volume projections, budgets, investment strategy. They will approve the underwriting team's plans, e.g. areas of business, countries, line limits, reinsurance programmes, and monitor the progress. This team is an essential general management one and should not attempt to interfere in the conduct of day-to-day risk acceptance—that is the underwriter's job (see Chapter 5).

Some underwriters may prefer not to be chief executive, in which case that function will be done by a managing director and it will be his job to leave the underwriter free to underwrite. However, the managing director and all members of the board must monitor the underwriting, must understand it, and must meet and know the underwriting staff. There is nothing worse than a prima donna underwriter with a room, or box, of deputies, working in isolation from the management. The whole company must be a team, knowing each other and working together.

Management should always insist on the objective of an underwriting or technical profit. On long-tail business the future developments of losses will almost inevitably prevent a technical profit being achieved, but the objective will have meant that the eventual loss is contained within the investment gain. Investment of funds and inflation of losses may, with luck and judgement, balance each other.

Line limits

As we have no income and will have no underwriting profits, at least for a few years, we shall have to set our line limits and exposure limits to any one disaster, as a function of our capital and investment income.

A capital of US$10,000,000 should permit us to accept for net account a maximum exposure on a single risk of around, say, 3% of our capital or US$300,000. This should not unduly call upon our capital and not make too great an inroad into the annual income of, say, $1,000,000 on that capital.

Now, applying this US$300,000 to different classes of underwriting:

(a) Pro rata property treaties

Our share in such treaties will be limited in two ways:

> First, by the maximum exposure on any one cession. For example, a first surplus five-line treaty with a risk exposure limit of US$10,000,000 and a maximum Probable Maximum Loss (PML) limit of US$2,500,000.
>
> We will be prepared to write a line of between 3% and perhaps 6%. Three per cent will expose us to US$300,000 maximum exposure any cession and US$75,000 exposure PML. Six per cent will expose us to US$600,000 maximum exposure any one cession and US$150,000 exposure PML.
>
> Our actual line will depend on the reliance we can place on the PML estimate of the ceding company, the volume of the treaty and, of course, its profitability. We would be unwise to write 12% in case the PML estimate proves to be unreliable.
>
> Secondly, by the volume of the treaty and its potential fluctuations in each annual period. If a treaty has a volume of, say, US$1,000,000 of net written income on a volatile class, with catastrophic exposures and a fluctuating past record, we might conclude that in any year the loss ratio could go to, say, 400% of the net written or US$4,000,000, in which case our line should be around 5% to 7.5% for an exposure of US$200,000 to US$300,000.
>
> Our line limits will be the lesser percentage line under the two assessments, which will mean that on a treaty with a big exposure per cession and a small volume, our lines will be determined by the cession limit, but on a treaty with a large volume by the potential annual maximum loss on that volume.

(b) Marine and aviation hull treaties

We can use exactly similar methods basing our lines on the maximum hull exposure to arrive at a maximum to us of not more than US$300,000 on any one bottom or on the volume and potential fluctuation. Here one must be careful as we have to take into account the accumulation exposure in a port or an airport and we will keep our maximum lines to US$200,000.

(c) Cargo treaties

The same philosophy but the governing risk exposure may not be the limit any one vessel but the warehouse or port accumulation.

(d) Personal accident treaties

Again the exposure limit must be determined not by the limit per person but by the accumulation limit in any one plane or coach.

(e) Hail and livestock and war treaties

The line limit here will be determined by the volume and the potential annual fluctuation, which may be very large indeed.

(f) Excess loss catastrophe contracts

Our basic limit of writing to lose not more than US$300,000 on any one exposure is still our guide, but we will have to be careful of some extra factors such as the possibility of two or more total losses in a year on lower layers and the accumulation factor between different contracts from the same markets or the same geographical areas.

I am in favour of classifying catastrophe excesses into three layers for your own underwriting purposes:

Lower layers—where you expect losses to happen.
Middle layers—where you will only get losses from major catastrophes.
Upper layers—where the exposure is to the super catastrophe.

Put it in terms of loss frequency:

Lower layers—every year to once in nine years
Middle layers—10 years to 39 years
Upper layers—40 years or over.

Put it in terms of premium rate on line, i.e. the percentage the contract premium bears to the occurrence limit of the cover:

Lower layers—10% or higher
Middle layers—10% to 4%

Upper layers—Under 4% rate on line.

Note: Lower layers should include any layer which has significant exposures on single risks from any class of business.

Now, our maximum commitment to any one programme, that is to all layers to one assured, should not exceed US$300,000. Obviously, it would not be wise to hazard that US$300,000 totally on a lower layer, but if we had no commitment except on an upper layer we could commit our maximum line on that layer alone.

So we could work to line limits as follows:

Lower layers around US$100,000
Lower and middle layers combined around US$200,000.

All layers not exceeding US$300,000.

We could give ourselves a little upwards flexibility to US$350,000 for use on very high top layers.

To give ourselves reasonable flexibility, and bearing in mind that our layers are arbitrary ones, we are going to use maximum line limits as follows:

Lower layers between US$100,000 and US$150,000
Middle layers and lower combined between US$150,000 and US$250,000.

All layers not exceeding US$350,000.

Now these line limits do not take into account accumulations that will inevitably happen between our different assureds writing the same type of business (and possibly the same original risks) in the same geographical areas. Where we know that such accumulations exist or are bound to exist (for example on LMX business or Texas wind business or North Sea oil rigs) then we may have to modify these line limits downwards to keep within our accumulation limits, but I will deal with this later on.

(g) Excess of loss layers with exposure to a single risk or risk excesses

That is, property, aviation, marine, miscellaneous accident layers, where we have single risk and PML exposures. Here our US$300,000 limit should be related to a reasonable maximum loss estimate to the contract itself during any annual period rather than to the occurrence or risk exposure of the contract.

For example, a contract for US$1,500,000 excess of US$500,000 each and every loss. Fully exposed to individual risk exposures in the year without an occurrence limit with an annual premium of, say, US$1,000,000 might well in a bad year have three total losses and we should base our line on, say, a limit of US$4,500,000 less US$1,000,000 or US$3,500,000 rather than US$1,500,000 and accept 8.25% and not 20%.

We are underwriting the *contract* as a risk exposure.

(h) Third party liability and motor excess contracts

I would suggest that these excess policies are subdivided into three basic layers—low, middle and high layers. Low layers are those layers that are exposed to losses for damage to a single individual, middle layers over this and top layers where it is impossible to envisage loss except in a major incident involving a considerable number of people or considerable damage to property.

Take a UK motor account in 1984. Awards in the range of £300,000 are now accepted. For individuals badly injured they will probably reach £500,000 for accidents occurring in 1984. Therefore, any excess of loss reinsurance substantially involved below £500,000 is a low excess. Top excesses must start at £3,000,000, all the rest are middle.

Take a UK motor account in 1989. Awards in the range of £800,000 are now accepted. For individuals badly injured they will probably reach £1,200,000 for accidents occurring in 1989 or 1990. Therefore any excess of loss reinsurance substantially involved below £1,200,000 must be a low excess. Top excesses must start at circa £5,000,000, all the rest are middle.

The difference between 1984 and 1989 shows that inflation of court awards in the last few years has outpaced normal inflation.

Our lines on top layers can be our maximum provided we are "clear" on the lower layers, and I suggest we use the same philosophy as we used for physical damage business but treating low layers not just as low layers, but also as underwriting layers. Thus, first calculate the maximum probable annual losses, less the premium, and base our lines on this. Then use our line guide of US$100,000 for low layers, US$200,000 on middle and lower and not exceeding US$350,000 overall.

(j) Excess aggregate or stop loss reinsurances

As a new company we are not going to underwrite general account stop losses but we may write them on specialist classes, hail on crops, weather, livestock, personal accident, medical. Here our lines will be geared as for catastrophe business but we will have two layers only and keep our lines cautious.

Low layers US$100,000 limit.
Top balance up to US$300,000.

Stop loss reinsurance is a very difficult class and we will only classify something as a high layer when we are very certain that the possibility of loss is extremely remote. For example, hurricane insurance on bananas or sugar crops can have loss ratios of 1000% where the original rates are, say, 2% and the crop suffers 30% damage. Thus, at stop loss of 500% loss ratio excess of 500% loss ratio can be a *low* layer.

(k) *Facultative R/Is*

Our line limit here can go to our maximum of US$300,000, but we shall treat this as a maximum limit per location and not as a PML limit; our PML maximum line will be US$100,000.

We must be cautious as our facultative lines are bound to clash with our treaty and contract commitments.

SUMMARY: MAXIMUM NET LINES

Around US$300,000 maximum.

Property treaties

Lesser of

>Exposure to one risk (not PML).
>Exposure to adverse annual experience on the volume of premium.

Marine and aviation hull treaties

US$200,000 any one vessel or aircraft.

Marine and aviation cargo treaties

US$200,000 reducing if known port or warehouse exposures.

Personal accident treaties

Exposure on maximum conveyance limit or loss.

Hail, livestock, war, miscellaneous accident treaties

Based on maximum annual fluctuation on the volume.

Excess catastrophe contracts

Low layers—US$100,000/US$150,000.
Middle layers—balance up to US$250,000.
Top layers—balance up to US$350,000.

Risk excess contracts

Based on maximum estimate of annual loss to the contract (i.e. maximum estimate of aggregate losses less premium).

Third party excess contracts

Low—not exceeding US$100,000.
Middle—balance up to US$250,000.
Top—balance up to US$350,000.

Excess aggregate

US$100,000 Low layers
US$300,000 All layers.

Facultative reinsurances

US$300,000 any one risk
US$100,000 P.M.L.

MAXIMUM PERCENTAGE LINES

As a new and fairly small reinsurer we must be very careful not to be carried away and write a big percentage share of a contract unless we are very, very certain of its quality and its reliability.

We will normally limit our share to a maximum of 10% of any one contract and only exceed this in special cases, and then only after group discussion (see Chapter 5). We will never be too greedy and write 100% or 50% of anything! We will need the support and wisdom of other sensible underwriters on the slip to correct our mistakes. We will never be infallible and "market" knowledge and caution is an essential part of underwriting.

CHAPTER 2

1983: SETTING THE SCENE 2—EXPENSES AND OTHER MATTERS

Our goal is to make an underwriting profit and to augment this with investment profit on the premium fund. This may not be possible in the early years because of our starting expenses and slow build-up of the premium fund. However, in order to make an underwriting profit we have got to control our expenses and this has an effect on the economic premium that we can write on an individual policy.

We shall set ourselves these normal maximum expense ratios for:

Pro rata treaties 2.5% of net premium.
Facultative reinsurances 5% of net premium (this might well be 10%).
Excess loss and stop loss 7.5% of net premium.

NB These expenses are our own overheads and do not include brokerage, taxes or other outgoings.

These will be calculated for each type of policy written to avoid writing uneconomic-sized premiums.

We have set expenses at these maximum levels so that we have some chance of making a profit on our underwriting.

It is simply no good writing a pro rata treaty account to make an underwriting profit if your expenses are, say, 7.5% because there will simply not be enough margin in the business to cover your expenses.

In my view expense ratios of 2.5%, 5% and 7.5% do give a reasonable chance of making a profit providing, of course, that we are selective in our underwriting, and if we aim at a maximum expense of this level on each contract written, our average expenses should come out at a lower figure.

We must now estimate the cost of taking each type of business on our books and of administering and processing it.

(1) First, a pro rata treaty; we need to cost these items:

    (a) Underwriter's time each year.
    (b) Recording details and setting up computer reference for accounts.
    (c) Agreeing six quarterly accounts.
    (d) Processing, say, six quarters' accounts.
    (e) Processing, say, three changes or endorsements per annum.

(f) Processing, say, three special settlements per annum (there may be many more!).

As follows:

(a) Assume that the underwriter's time costs US$80,000 per annum. He actually underwrites 20 hours a week for 40 weeks. Cost US$100 per hour. Each treaty takes an hour per annum. Cost US$100.
(b) Say, US$50.
(c) Say, US$50.
(d), (e) and (f) Twelve entries at US$12.50: cost—say, US$150.

Total cost US$350 per treaty per annum. Round this up to US$375.

Therefore, our minimum economic net premium on a pro rata treaty should be around $15,000, of which 2.5% expenses gives US$375.

(2) Facultative reinsurance

Underwriting time six minutes	= US$10
Processing four times per year at US$10	US$40
Total	US$50
Minimum premium US$1000 5% expenses =	US$50

N.B. This means that on a facultative reinsurance where the net rate is .10% our written line must not be less than US$1,000,000 to be economic with 10% expenses, $2,000,000.

We obviously have a problem, which we will discuss later.

(3) Excess of loss/stop loss

Underwriting time 15 minutes	= US$25
Processing five times per year at US$10	US$50
Total	US$75
Minimum premium US$1000 7.5% expenses =	US$75

N.B. On a top excess at a *net* rate of .50% our minimum economic line will be US$200,000.

Each operation will have to do its own calculation and the above may be totally unrealistic for some companies but bear in mind:

(a) We have not costed the business we decline.
(b) That every year some business will require a lot of time if things go wrong.
(c) If treaty accounts cannot be agreed on first submission then more time is spent.
(d) No allowance is made for our own reinsurance costs.
(e) No allowance is made for general overheads.

(f) Our costings are *minimal* both as to the cost of an item and the number of items.

Nevertheless we have arrived at these conclusions—that the absolute minimum premiums for which we can economically take on any single reinsurance are:

Treaties	US$15,000 per annum
Facultative Reinsurances	US$1,000 per item
Excess Loss and Stop Loss	US$1,000 per contract.

Now let us study this in relation to the line limits set out in Chapter 1.

On pro rata treaties a minimum of US$15,000 should not inhibit us too much. On a treaty with a volume of US$1,500,000 per annum net of ceding commission we can accept as little as a 1% line but it will be pointless to fiddle around writing 1% or 2% lines on treaties with a volume of US$100,000 or US$200,000 per annum. We either write 7.5% or decline them.

On facultative reinsurances we will have a major problem. Our maximum net line is $300,000, which, at a .10% rate, will produce a premium of $300, which will be completely uneconomic. Therefore, if we are going to underwrite a facultative reinsurance account we will either have to obtain reinsurance protection ourselves, to increase our gross lines, join in a pool with others to make the operation viable, or take a quota share of someone else's operations.

Let us assume that we take out a three-line first surplus and obtain an overriding commission of 5% for our expenses. If we accept US$1,200,000 on a risk where the net rate is .08% the premium is US$960, on which our cost will be US$50, or 5%, which is just economical. Provided the cost of ceding to the treaty is covered by the overriding commission we will receive from our reinsurers, then we should be economic—just!

If we are going into the facultative reinsurance business we will need a three-line first surplus treaty or a 75% quota share treaty, or possibly some combination of treaty and specific excess protection on a risk basis so that we have a capacity of around US$1,200,000 on the low rated risks.

An alternative is to find someone else to do it for us and to take a quota share from them, or go into a pool with a pool capacity of US$1,200,000 and our share being 25%. We will consider this a little later when we have discussed our excess and stop loss reinsurances.

ON EXCESS OF LOSS AND STOP LOSS REINSURANCES

There will be top layers on, for example, third party excesses, personal accident excesses and others where the net rate on line is below 1%. For example, a line of US$300,000 at 25c, less 15%, will produce a net premium to us of around US$600—uneconomic. Also there will be many occasions where we cannot write US$300,000 because we have lower layers, or concentrations exist.

Therefore, we will need extra capacity to cover our excess loss and stop loss business as well as our facultative writings.

OUR OUTWARDS TREATY PROGRAMME

We have established that:

> A quota share or surplus treaty is required to allow us to write economic-sized lines on facultative reinsurance and excess loss and stop loss reinsurance.

We have the choice of taking out a quota share, a surplus, possibly an excess protection or a combination of any two or all three of the above. A quota share is economic to operate but we will have to cede away a big percentage of our premiums to obtain the capacity we need. An excess of loss approach will be unstable and difficult to cost until we have several years' experience. It is not suitable for a new account.

A first surplus makes amore sense but its administration will be costly as each cession will require a separate calculation of premium.

If we are a reinsurer obliged, or under pressure, to accept 100%, or a large share of our cedant's business, for example a national reinsurance company expected to assume the majority of local business, or a company dealing directly with our clients, then our outwards reinsurance programme may have to be designed to allow us to write a gross line on all classes of business that is several times our net line. If this is so, then we will need a sizeable retrocession treaty and this will best be done as a surplus. We could envisage a five-line first surplus pool which could be used to give reciprocity back to our reassureds, plus an additional five-line second surplus retrocession treaty ceded to international markets.

Such retrocession treaties could be arranged for different classes, e.g. property treaties, facultative acceptances, third party excess, marine hulls.

The overriding commissions obtained would have to cover at least part of our overheads in writing the business plus the cost to us of running the treaty or pool.

So far as we are concerned we are a reinsurance company in a market place and can select the size of our line, and therefore we will try to obtain the best of all worlds by taking out a graded quota share where we have only four options in making a cession.

> *Option one:* to cede half a line or 33.33% of our gross acceptance.
> *Option two:* to cede one line or 50% of our gross acceptance.
> *Option three:* to cede two lines or 66.66% of our gross acceptance.
> *Option four:* to cede three lines or 75% of our gross acceptance.

Our maximum net line limits will be:

US$300,000 any one risk for both facultative and excess loss.

This will give us the capacity we need of up to US$1,200,000 any one risk. We will code each risk at the time we accept it with the appropriate cession code, i.e. no reinsurance cession, or 1, 2, 3 or 4 as above.

Our whole accounting of premiums and losses will then be bulked in four quota share that which can each be accounted quarterly without bordereaux.

Our outwards reinsurance treaty will read something like this:

Obligatory treaty:

To take half a net line or 33.33% quota share of all risks coded 1, or
to take one net line or 50% quota share of all risks coded 2, or
to take two net lines or 66.66% quota share of all risks coded 3, or
to take three net lines or 75% quota share of all risks coded 4.

Maximum cession per line US$300,000 any one risk, i.e. maximum cession per risk for

Code 1   US$150,000
Code 2   US$300,000
Code 3   US$600,000
Code 4   US$900,000

Quarterly accounts. Quarterly settlements of balance.
Special settlements of losses over US$100,000.
Outstanding claims advance as original.
ONR—5% override (2.50% might do) 20% profit commission (5% expenses).

CHAPTER 3

1983: SETTING THE SCENE
3—ACCUMULATION AND REINSURANCE PROTECTION

NOTE

The type of reinsurance we can purchase, and its price, will greatly depend on the market available. In 1983 that retrocession market was tough. In a tough market we will have to accept what we can get. However, my philosophy as regards outwards reinsurance is that we should only purchase reinsurance for a specific underwriting purpose and not use reinsurance to write for overriding commission, nor purchase reinsurance that we do not really need just because we can obtain it at "cheap" terms. I believe that it is a shortsighted policy to deliberately use soft reinsurance markets. Therefore, I am proposing a simple reinsurance programme and our policy will be to underwrite our gross account, our net account, and our reinsured account, to produce a technical profit to us and our reinsurers.

CATASTROPHIC PROTECTION, OUR GENERAL EXCESS PROGRAMME

We have set out maximum net lines on single risks at $300,000 or 3% of our capital and around 30% of our earnings on that capital. We now need to consider at what point we should protect ourselves from catastrophic losses, or losses which could arise from accumulations of single very large exposures. This figure should not be more than 7.50% of our capital but we must bear in mind that we can have several losses in a year that we may have to co-insure on our own protection and to pay reinstatement premiums on any losses we collect. A deductible of 5% or £500,000 will be high enough.

The exact layers we will buy will depend on the availability of reinsurance and the amount of cover we need to meet our accumulation exposures. We might suggest coverage as follows:

Reinsurance in US$000

    Layer 1: 1,500 excess of 500 each and every loss occurrence. (A 1,000 deductible is perhaps more realistic.)
    Layer 2: 3,000 excess of 2,000 each and every loss occurrence.

Layer 3: 5,000 excess of 5,000 each and every loss occurrence.

The purchase of layer three being delayed until we need it (see Chapter 4).

We will want 100% cover if possible (but can accept 90%) and will probably have to accept one reinstatement per annum on each layer. We will need an aggregate extension clause so that our own recoveries will follow our commitments on third party or other policies where the protection is granted by us on an aggregate basis. (Aggregate extensions ceased in 1986 after asbestos losses.)

OTHER GENERAL REINSURANCES

We should consider:

(a) The possibility of buying a second reinstatement policy on our first general layer for US$1,500,000 excess of US$500,000. In other words, a policy for the third total loss on that layer. If this is inexpensive it will be better to have it before we suffer a loss on the layer of US$1,500,000 excess of US$500,000. But we may not need this policy until we see how our accumulations build up.

(b) The possibility of purchasing a layer of, say, US$200,000 excess of US$300,000 each and every loss but only to pay when loss or losses to that layer exceed US$200,000 in the aggregate in any annual period. This means that our protection on our first loss comes in at US$500,000, and on our second major loss in the year at US$300,000, which will help us to conserve our capital.

THIRD PARTY REINSURANCE

Here we are concerned with our exposure on long-tail business. We should certainly reinsure our third party business including any third party element of our inwards global policies, and our protection must have an aggregate extension clause, at the lowest possible fixed deductible. If we can buy, for example, US$400,000 excess of US$100,000 or even US$450,000 excess of US$50,000 each and every loss with an aggregate extension clause, we should do so. We may have to pay 30% of our third party income for it but even so it will be very valuable to us in our long-tail liabilities. This policy will be underlying to our general excess programme.

MARINE HULL, CARGO AND OIL RIGS

We will need to include these in our general excess of loss protection if economic or marketable, otherwise it may be better to take out a specific excess of loss protection for our marine account and our rig account.

The deductible of US$500,000 identical to our main deductible would be reasonable and we shall need sufficient cover to protect us against a major port disaster or a natural disaster such as a hurricane or earthquake. A protection for, say, US$2,500,000 excess of US$500,000 any one disaster should be reasonable. With our line limits of US$200,000 any one hull or cargo this will protect us for 15 times our maximum exposure excess of twice our maximum. If we purchase this specific marine excess then our general excess should cover marine business with the marine cover inuring to the benefit of the general excess, thus limiting our loss to US$500,000 in a combined disaster.

OTHER REINSURANCES

These are the essential protections we shall need. There may be others—for example:

(a) specific protection for LMX business and rig business when we write some;
(b) stop loss protection for war and political risks if obtainable;
(c) stop loss protection for crop hail business;

but these can wait until we see how our account will develop.

STOP LOSS REINSURANCE

I must here say a word about stop loss protection for our whole account. One is tempted to purchase stop loss protection to guarantee that we do not lose money on our underwriting.

This can be a very dangerous reinsurance to take out even if it can be purchased at a reasonable price. The trouble is, that like all cosy protections, it can lull one to sleep. Reinsurance is a hard world and one needs always to have the sharp, cold incentive of making an underwriting profit gross and net. It is very easy for this to become blurred if you know that you are protected from your own underwriting results. In addition, if you have a claim against your stop loss reinsurers you may be unable to renew the reinsurance and you then have to run off your account without it.

However, a modest layer of stop loss protection in our early years is a nice sleep at night protection.

We could try and obtain protection for, say, 90% of 20% excess of 105% net loss ratio. If possible a three-year firm contract to see us through our first three years. We will need to make sure our minimum deductible, particularly for year one, is low enough so that if our income is low we will not be penalised. Whether we purchase it will depend on its price and the security of the reinsurers. In practice we could not obtain this cover.

ACCUMULATION EXPOSURES

We now have to consider our underwriting policy with particular regard to accumulation exposures. In the international reinsurance field, particularly that based on major international centres such as London, it is very easy to build up very heavy accumulation exposures to a single disaster or a period of general bad experience.

We propose to write a general excess of loss reinsurance account to *direct writing companies* throughout the world. Accumulations on these can be controlled by area fairly easily, as we shall discuss. If we, in addition, write excess of loss reinsurances to worldwide reinsurance companies and Lloyd's syndicates who themselves are writing similar excess of loss business, then our exposures will be much more difficult to control and we may have to assume that all such contracts are exposed in every area of the world.

In addition, we may find that we are underwriting back part of our own reinsurance protection. In other words, if a reinsurance company writes our excess protection and we write his, we can find ourselves swapping our own losses back and forth and this can happen indirectly through retrocession.

We are, therefore, going to confine our underwriting to excess of loss reinsurances of direct writing companies and to write reinsurance accounts where they write proportional business only, e.g. a first surplus treaty. We will only protect reinsurance companies provided the contract contains an excess of loss reinsurance clause. London LMX business will also be excluded except for specialised business that does not present an accumulation hazard.

Having said that, if we judge the market conditions to be favourable enough for a profit to be made on such business, i.e. there is a great shortage of capacity worldwide and rates are favourable, e.g. just after a major disaster, then we will consider making a special "book" of such business. We would underwrite net lines or protect this book by a separate reinsurance protection.

EXPOSURE CONTROLS

To return, then, to the control of our excess loss reinsurance book of business from direct writing companies, we have suggested a breakdown into three categories:

- Low layers
- Middle layers
- High layers

In addition, we shall need to classify our business into exposure areas. These, of course, can be very detailed and, of course, will vary with our position in the world. We are going to use very broad areas for our non-marine property business:

(1) USA—Texas, Oklahoma
(2) USA—California and West Coast
(3) USA—Louisiana, Florida and South East
(4) USA—East Coast and New England
(5) USA—Mid-West
(6) Canada
(7) Europe
(8) Mexico, Venezuela, Caribbean and Central America
(9) Japan
(10) Rest of the World
(11) USA and Canada General
(12) Rest of the World General

Most contracts we write will fall reasonably into one category or into category 11 or 12. If, of course, we are writing heavily in, say, Europe, a breakdown between France, Germany and Scandinavia and United Kingdom would make sense or the US could well be divided into eight or nine different zones, not five only. Now we will have to keep records of our liabilities in each area for low, medium and high excess. Our liability in California and the West Coast will be the total of category two plus category 11.

Using these liabilities we must estimate their susceptibility to loss. We would use a simple suggestion that all low layers are 100% subject, middle layers 60% and upper layers 40%. There will always be some contracts that are not fully exposed in some areas. If we are well organised we can analyse our exposures more accurately. One method is by market share. If a company has, say, 5% of the property business in Texas then an insured loss of US$3,000,000,000 in Texas should cost that company US$150,000,000. In most areas of the world outside the United States we may use a different approach, for example, Japan.

The potential loss from a real major Japanese earthquake affecting say, Zone 5, and possible neighbouring zones, is so great that we may have to consider all layers, lower, middle and upper, in classification nine as fully exposed. On the other hand, classification 12 may be lightly exposed except for certain known companies who operate in Japan or who have substantial Japanese inwards treaties.

As we take on business these liabilities have to be recorded and PMLs estimated. We have suggested that we purchase total reinsurance protection up to US$5,000,000 initially. Assume we write:

US$000 category 12 totals
    20 lower layers   2,000
    10 middle layers   1,500
    20 top layers   4,000

Then we have a picture like this:

```
         2,000   100% subject = 2,000
    plus 1,500    60% subject =   900
    plus 4,000    40% subject = 1,600
```

Total estimated exposure
to one loss   4,500

With a global protection for US$4,500,000 excess of US$500,000 each and every loss, we have US$500,000 spare for any specific area liabilities. Once our liabilities start to reach these figures we shall have to consider purchasing more protection, i.e. taking out a further layer for, say, US$5,000,000 excess of US$5,000,000.

Bear in mind that we will also have additional liabilities on facultative reinsurances, treaty writing, marine hulls and cargoes and even on personal accident and third party layers.

We will have to relate our reinsurance costs carefully to the business we assume. Taking our example above, our premium income might be:

US$000

```
    Lower layers of   2,000 produce   250 premium per annum
    Medium layers of  1,500 produce    75 premium per annum
    Higher layers of  4,000 produce    80 premium per annum
                              Total   405
```

We need therefore to develop income spread over all categories to provide us with an income to afford the protection we desire. If we blithely pay US$500,000 for our protection of US$4,500,000 excess of US$500,000, we are going to be in trouble.

Our accumulations on other classes need booking and controlling too, for example marine hulls and cargo excesses, and here the treaty liabilities will be significant. Our aviation liabilities will be a mixture of facultative, treaty and excess. Third party has not, until recently, presented an accumulation exposure comparable to physical damage, but two factors must be taken into account.

First, the third party and professional indemnity claims, e.g. architects' indemnity, which might arise from a major earthquake or the liability for causing a flood or starting a fire.

Secondly, the incidence of industrial or latent disease, e.g. asbestosis or deafness, pollution and environmental claims, may involve many insurance companies over long periods of time. Therefore, we must record our aggregate liabilities on third party excesses and these liabilities may have to be expressed, not as liabilities for any one loss, but as the aggregate annual exposure possible to us from a number of claims.

CHAPTER 4

1983: REINSURANCE SYSTEMS AND CONTROLS

Our systems will have to provide us with:

(1) Underwriting data

(a) A record of the underwriting data and the information available for each piece of business accepted. This must include our own references relating to it. It must be in an imperishable form which can be kept for years. The record must also include the underwriter's comments made when he accepted the business, i.e. *why* he accepted, with similar notes on renewals. It is absolutely vital that all business on which we are on risk is recorded by us *when accepted*.

(b) A record of business seen and quoted or declined, including comments and the reasons *why* it was not accepted.

I stress here the importance of the notes and comments and information. These will be of great help in future years if problems arise on any piece of business.

(c) Filing for copies of slips, the information supplied, correspondence, wordings and underwriting notes and aides memoire.

(2) Accounts

A proper accounting system with each client and a system to check unpaid and overdue settlements. I do not propose to dwell on this. The underwriter will need to know who pays promptly and who does not. In addition, he will often need to know the payment position, say, on premiums due, before paying losses.

(3) Claims

A method of recording settled claims and claims expenses. A method of recording outstanding losses, and here we will need to have a method of recording the estimates given by our cedants and our own acceptance of these or, if we do not agree these, our own estimates of the outstanding liabilities.

Where no estimate is given by a cedant we will have to make estimates of our own. It is important also to remember the importance (particularly in the USA) of estimating for claims expenses, e.g. lawyers' fees.

(4) Outwards reinsurances

Use of our outwards treaty

Where a cession is made, this will be recorded when the original business is written by code reference. This reference will be repeated on all documentation. All premiums and paid claims can then be accounted and settled with our reinsurers quarterly in bulk. We will need a system to advise them of outstanding losses to the treaty.

Outwards facultative reinsurance

We will need a system of individual advice of premiums and additional premiums and claims paid and claims outstanding. They will be expensive to administer and account and we must keep outwards facultative reinsurance of our account to a minimum.

Excess of loss outwards protection

We must record each major claim separately in our claims records with the note of each contract giving us a loss from that claim. This will have to include paid and outstanding advices. Once the total looks like involving our reinsurers they will be kept advised according to the contract conditions.

It is important that treaty losses be included. This can be very time-consuming and one may never have the actual details in the original treaty accounts. Some arrangement is necessary with our reinsurers so that endless time and money is not spent on chasing possible reinsurance recoveries for small treaty losses.

Note: In keeping our own statistics it is important that our statistics are kept both on a gross basis (i.e. before reinsurances are deducted) and on a net basis (after deduction of reinsurances). We shall have more to say about this below when we consider underwriting statistics.

(5) Recording liabilities for excess of loss and stop loss inwards business

We will need a system to record our liabilities net and gross of treaty and facultative reinsurance as set out above:

i.e. by type of business, e.g. property, marine hull
by areas
by low, middle and high layers.

(6) Underwriting statistics

In addition to proper accounting we are going to need statistics for control and analysis of our underwriting. These statistics will be produced for our whole account and broken down into different categories. They will be kept on a year of attachment basis. That is to say, any piece of business with an inception date in, say, 1985 is 1985 account business. Additional premiums received on such business in, say, 1988 or claims first advised in 2001 will still be 1985 business.

Only by keeping statistics in this way will we ever be able to keep track of our underwriting. Each attachment year or year of account will, in our underwriting statistics, be kept open *for ever.*

I am suggesting one method only of keeping statistics. I am sure it can be improved upon but any system should allow the underwriter and management to review monthly the progress on the business on a total account basis both gross and net of reinsurance and to review it on a gross basis after deduction of facultative and treaty reinsurance for each major class. Periodically, quarterly or yearly the account can be reviewed in greater detail.

In addition, if these reviews throw up problems or, say, a very good result, it must be possible for the underwriter to analyse it from his statistics. Furthermore, these statistics by categories will allow us to track the pattern both of premium receipts and loss payments. This will be vital to us in building up past statistics for estimating our outstanding liability reserves, particularly our Incurred But Not Reported (IBNR) reserves.

Our categories, too, can be used to determine the results obtained by one of our individual underwriters, always presuming that we shall have a number of people underwriting particular segments of our account. We therefore need:

> First, certain individual pieces of business such as treaties will have to be given a unique reference so that we keep individual accounts on an attachment year basis (the anniversary date of a treaty being a new attachment date). We need this to keep our records of the treaty experience to compare it with our cedants' figures and also to make sure that we receive accounts and payments on time and to keep track of portfolio transfers and reserve items. It may also be wise to include certain excess of loss working covers, pools and any agency or binding covers, i.e. to keep individual statistics on each contract.
>
> Secondly, all our business, including treaties, should be classified. I suggest in three ways:

—by the territory
—by the class of insurance (e.g. marine hulls)
—by method of reinsurance (e.g. first surplus treaty).

With three distinct codes we can have great flexibility and, of course, we can amalgamate figures produced as we wish so we are not faced with a large printout of very small categories.

(a) Territories

These will vary with your own locality. I suggest these for a worldwide account written from London.

Code 00 Worldwide, excluding USA
     01 USA
     02 Canada
     03 UK
     04 France
     05 Germany and Scandinavia
     06 Rest of Europe
     07 Central and South America
     08 Australia
     09 Japan
     10 Middle East
     99 Rest of World

(b) Class

Code 00 Property, excluding personal accident
     01 Liability, excluding motor
     02 Motor
     03 Personal accident
     04 Workmen's compensation and employers' liability
     05 War and contingency
     06 Marine hulls
     07 Marine cargo
     08 Oil rigs
     09 Aviation hulls
     10 Aviation liabilities
     99 Miscellaneous

(c) Type of reinsurance

Code 01 Facultative reinsurance
     02 Quota share treaties

03 Surplus treaties
04 Facultative obligatory treaties
05 Underwriting or risk excesses including loss cost and burning costs
06 Low level excess of loss
07 Medium level excess of loss
08 High level excess of loss
09 Stop loss
10 Pools, agency, binders
99 Miscellaneous

This will give you over 1,000 categories—far too many to look at periodically but you can look at them by major class and then, if your marine cargo is dreadful, you can easily ascertain the area and the type of contract that is causing the problem. Or you can simply reduce them. For example, aviation liability business may need only two territorial classifications—00 and 01.

These underwriting statistics must be reviewed periodically, say once a month or once a quarter, but no one can take in more than, say, 20 to 30 sets of statistics. So keep your normal printouts to this number and then ask the computer to produce more if you need to analyse any in greater detail. Each category will show premiums received against losses paid and can, if you want it, include losses outstanding. At least these should be included at the close of each year and possibly, if available, quarterly.

The next problem is one of currencies. To keep such statistics in all the original currencies is absurd. Certainly they should be in your own, and perhaps one or two others. For example, if 30% of your business is in US dollars, you ought to keep statistics in US dollars (see Chapter 5).

Another problem is: should these be on a gross basis, i.e. before or after reinsurance? It is my view that they are best kept net of facultative reinsurances and net of your outwards treaty, but that general protections, e.g. a third party excess protection or a general catastrophe protection, should not be deducted.

This gives a good picture of your underwriting class record and a good idea of the run-off statistics and does not involve allocating reinsurance premium or loss recoveries between categories.

Whatever you do, be consistent and note all records with any changes you make and changes forced on you: for example, a major change in exchange rates.

One main purpose of these statistics on a year of attachment basis is to allow us to track the development of any classes on each attachment year as that year develops in time. To do this we shall use a "triangulation" of results. For example:

Our category 03 04 06
UK Motor Low level excess

Year of attachment	\multicolumn{10}{c}{Calendar years of progression}	Est Final LR
	1	2	3	4	5	6	7	8	9	10	
1983	20	40	60	100	110						130
1984	30	50	70	100							120
1985	10	30	50								100
1986	15	40									110
1987	20										?

Position at end of 1987 shown

THOUGHTS ON COMPUTERS

The advance of computers continues and continues and continues and most of my readers will be more familiar with them than I ever was.

There are, however, certain words of warning. Do not get too dependent on one source, either your own parent firm or a bureau. Alternatively, small computers for your underwriting statistics may make sense.

Do not spend too long looking at screens; no one knows yet what effect they will have on your health, or your sanity, and maybe the next but one industrial disease will be "screenitis".

Do not let the computer replace your brain cells. Underwriting is not just statistics, it is part common sense, part statistics and future projections of them, part assessment of people and part an art form.

Two thousand years ago the Celtic people in these islands could not write. The laws and knowledge of these islands was contained in memories of individuals. The memory of our pre-literate ancestors astounded the Greeks and Romans. The function of memory tended to wither once writing was used.

In this century adding machines, calculators and computers are replacing mental arithmetic. The ability of the Edwardian brain to calculate is fast disappearing.

My advice to any young underwriter is first to cultivate the memory and secondly to cultivate the ability to do mental arithmetic. A good underwriter, like a good bookmaker, ought always to have a calculator within his own head that will instinctively tell him of the odds or probabilities of any proposition, and a memory of past mistakes, and past examples, that automatically guides him through new propositions, which in many cases are only rehashes of past propositions.

And lastly, writing something down in your own fair hand is one of the best ways of sorting out a problem and this applies to writing down the mathematics itself as well as to the writing of a slip or a wording.

Never rush a decision if you can spend a few more minutes or a few more hours in analysing it mentally with your own written notes. The old adage that "time spent in reconnaissance is never wasted" is as true in reinsurance as it was on the battlefield and, after all, reinsurance today is a battlefield.

CHAPTER 5

1983: OTHER REINSURANCE UNDERWRITING PROBLEMS

A. RESERVING

The interpretation of statistics for reserving purposes is beyond the scope of this workbook. In general terms the first few years of a reinsurance account is a period of uncertainty. On short-tail business, property, marine cargoes, aviation hull, personal accident and war, your results will become pretty definite on the USA side once the fourth quarter treaty accounts are processed. On the non-USA side, once portfolio transfers have been made under your treaties. In other words, towards the end of year two you will have a good idea of year one's results.

On medium-tail, e.g. contributing reinsurance of motor, workers' compensation and employers' liability, marine hull and aviation liabilities, it will take at least three years for claims to be advised and estimated (rather longer on marine hull) before you will be able to calculate your own results.

On long-tail, e.g. excess of loss on above classes outside the USA, it will take at least five years. On the very long-tail, such classes as USA excess casualty and excess products, the pattern will not emerge for ten years or longer.

We must therefore not get excited if, after three years, we have a very low settled loss ratio on long-tail and very long-tail business. It gives us very little guide as to our ultimate results.

Therefore, on these classes, our reserving policy must be to keep the balance between premium and paid losses as our Incurred But Not Reported (IBNR) reserve, adding to our investment gain on these balances, or, alternatively, one must assume a final loss ratio for the year of account in question and one's reserve is the difference between that loss ratio and your paid losses to date.

The assumed loss ratio should never be less than 100%, and in many cases should be considerably greater than 100%, e.g. on US casualty business for the years 1978 and 1983 inclusive an assumed loss ratio of 150% would not be unreasonable.

Only when we can be sure of the pattern of settlement can we estimate the final results within a certain range. This pattern of settlement on these classes may best be seen graphically.

The problems of asbestos and pollution liabilities only increase the difficulties of reserving long-tail business in any meaningful way. They can only be done as a percentage of one's total gross liability based on loss probabilities. They cannot be reviewed or estimated by progression graphs. From these gross liabilities one's projected reinsurance recoveries can be deducted, making allowance for restrictions in collections due to limited reinstatements and non-collection due to disputes or insolvency.

Typical long-tail settlement pattern

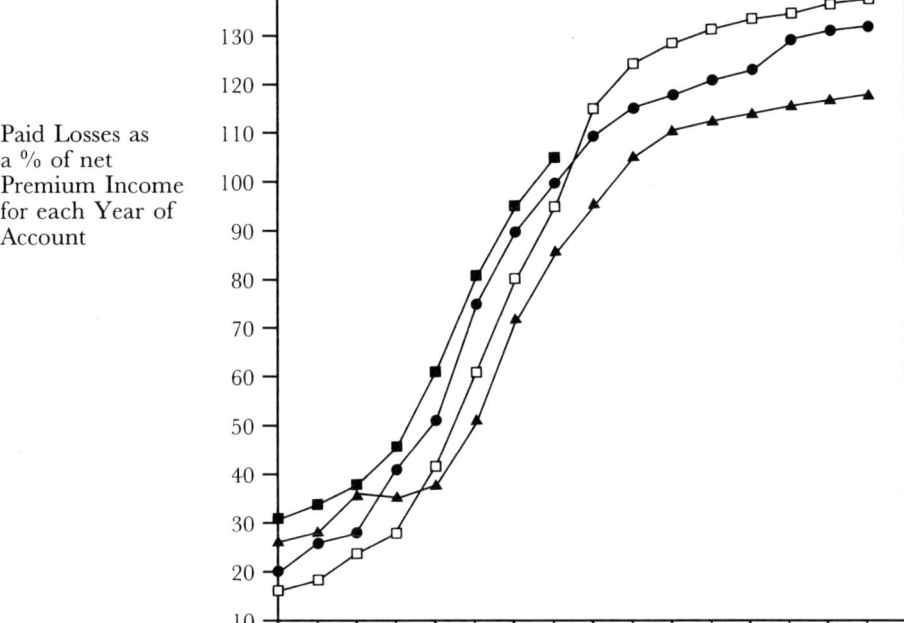

■ 1976 Account   ▲ 1970 Account   ● 1969 Account   □ 1968 Account

1968 Account Paid Losses FINAL 132%
1969 Account Paid Losses FINAL 138%
1970 Account Paid Losses FINAL 118%
1976 Account Paid Losses FINAL 147%

For each year of account the settlement percentage is plotted at the end of year one, year two, etc. to infinity.

The graph line for each year of account will gradually level out and will approach the final settlement at infinity.[1]

---

1. The problems of asbestosis, latent disease and pollution play havoc with such curves as the very delayed advices and settlements cause kinks in the curves, even 20 or so years later.

I have plotted four years of account as examples of a typical long-tail account, i.e. 1968, 1969 and 1970 plus the 1976 account.

The final results of the three earlier years will be pretty definite unless some unknown factor is still to affect them, e.g. asbestosis. Normally with a long-tail account, these curves acquire a shape somewhere around the sixth to ninth year of settlement. This means that the settlement patterns of the early years, i.e. years one to five, can mean very little and cannot be used to predict a final result. But once the shape takes form it can be used to predict, e.g. to predict 1976 result after eight years.

Once the final results of a year can be estimated then the reserve for outstanding losses is the difference between that result and the amount paid to date.

This reserve must be increased by a factor to take care of unknown future inflation, adjusted for currency movements, and must be increased by the estimated cost of running a claims organisation to service and pay the outstanding claims, and this will be a very sizeable amount and itself adjusted for future increases in premises cost and wages.

NB This reserve should be calculated on a gross and net basis and the net result increased by a factor to take account of failure of one's reinsurers to pay both outstanding losses and IBNR.

To summarise therefore:

Short-tail business

A proper recording of your outstanding liabilities, including return premiums, portfolio transfers, adjustments under self-rated contracts, profit commissions and sliding scales adjustments, will enable you to make proper reserves using a reasonable adjustment for IBNR after 24 months of each annual account.

Medium-tail business

The same process can be carried out after perhaps 48 months.

Long-tail business

On long-tail business, and the early year on the medium-tail, other methods must be used. These are:
- (a) Use of outstanding losses inflated to take account of inflation likely during the period that claims will take to settle plus an IBNR factor based on these known outstanding losses.
- (b) Assumption of a final estimated loss ratio based on market experience and "feel" of each year of account. This loss ratio to be not less than 100% and reserve to be difference between estimated loss ratio and paid losses to date.

(c) Reserve to be 100% of premiums less paid losses to date plus interest received to date on the premium balance.
(d) Use of projections, graphical or otherwise, to predict reserve from your own past statistics or market statistics.
(e) On long-tail classes an assumed probable loss on one's exposures.

The reserve to be used should be in theory the largest of the above four or at least a top average. To this figure must be added:

(a) The cost of processing and settling the liabilities itself adjusted for inflation.
(b) A fluctuation reserve for the unknown—say, asbestosis, future super inflation, etc.
(c) Cost of non-collection from your reinsurers.
(d) Cost of disputes with your reinsurers.

On long-tail business this will mean reserves of many times the annual volume of premium.

Discounting

These reserves will not be discounted for future interest earnings on the reserves themselves.

If the reserve is conservatively calculated and includes the increases made above, particularly the cost of running off a claims department, then there is justification to discount. *But*, that discounting must be conservative and the assumed rate of interest used should be around 2.5% to 4%—never, in my view, more than 6%.

Of course, in dealing with Lloyd's "reinsurances to close" or other portfolio reinsurances, these as commercial reinsurances should be, and ought to be, discounted and may be discounted at slightly higher figures again only if the outstanding loss reserves have been increased as suggested above.

Anyone wishing to research this further should refer to specialist publications[2] or a good actuary in the non-life field.

But before you start underwriting, make certain that you have established your systems to produce premiums, paid losses, outstanding losses for each class of long-tail and medium-tail business on a year of account basis by each major currency gross and net of reinsurance for ever.

B. CURRENCY

It is a good practice to match your liabilities with assets and your reserves should be held in a matching currency.

---

2. *Financial Analysis of a Reinsurance Office* by David Craighead, available from IRRG, deals with reserving and discounting in greater detail.

If a European reinsurer is writing a significant volume of Canadian business then you ought to hold part of your funds in Canadian dollars to cover or match your Canadian liabilities. This may be done for you either by authorities requiring deposits or trust funds or by your cedants demanding them. If not, you do it yourself and keep assets in major currencies to match your liabilities.

C. INVESTMENT OF THE PREMIUM FUND AND RESERVES

An underwriter must have some say in this and he should be in agreement with investment strategy. The funds are his policyholder's money, which must match his liabilities to policyholders. As in theory these claims can be paid at any time such funds must be invested in readily realisable assets and, of course, well spread so that a fluctuation in one's assets will not affect this liability.

In the early years of an insurance operation, funds must be kept liquid. Only when we can reasonably establish our settlement pattern can our investment programme become longer to match in part that settlement pattern.

D. CASH FLOW CONTROL

Holding cash is a vital part of the game. An underwriter must always take the payment factor into account when writing business. Similarly, if reserves are asked for on treaties one must reduce ceding commissions or acquire realistic interest rates. Deposit premiums on excess business should be as near the 100% estimated earnings as possible and paid at inception.

It is quite vital that before you start underwriting you and your accounts department set up some system to see that payments are made to you on time.

E. DECISION-TAKING

Underwriting is a constant process of assessment and decision-taking: some people relish taking decisions, others are worried by them. They will not make underwriters, but the support team. Those who like decision-taking can only be trained to it by practice and they have actually to underwrite on their own and take decisions themselves without someone holding their hand. So, if you are an underwriter, train and let your deputies take decisions and let them underwrite parts of your account provided you review every day what they have done. Which leads me on to my next paragraph.

Control of day-to-day underwriting

There is no foolproof way by which management can control the actual process of risk acceptance. The judgement of the underwriter has to be the final arbiter and the experience, intelligent foresight and character of the underwriter are the vital elements. However, no person is infallible and the power and responsibility of the underwriter can warp judgements and can cause people to think they are infallible, or at least better than they are. Flattery exercised by brokers and cedants can also warp judgements.

Management can set line limits and underwriting instructions and can, of course, monitor results on the lines we have suggested, but analysing results, vital though it is, can only happen well after the event.

Many sound underwriting operations have been ruined by an underwriter taking on bad business, writing too large a commitment, being simply carried away by the excitement or intricacy of solving a technical problem, having a temporary lapse of memory or being susceptible to flattery or drink!

It is vital, in my view, that at the end of every day, or better still, in the clear light of the next morning, all the business taken on or renewed the previous day is discussed *risk by risk* by a group of people—the underwriter and his deputies or assistants.

The actual person who accepted the business should explain why he wrote it to his peers, and colleagues, and they should question him. If the group feels that the risk is wrong, or the line accepted too heavy, then corrective steps can be taken there and then and the underwriting records so marked.

This has several beneficial effects. First, an individual knowing he has to answer to his peers, exercises more caution. Secondly, the person who accepted the business has a chance of a second think, and lastly, the underwriting team members learn from each other and develop trust and understanding as a team.

It is vital that the underwriter, the boss, however powerful his personality and his experience, disciplines himself to accept the questioning and the control of his junior colleagues.

A person who is not prepared to do this may be brilliant but he can be a very real potential danger and I am not prepared to employ him or trust my money to him.

In addition, the underwriter's job is to underwrite, not to manage the company. He must not take on work or outside activities that prevent him underwriting daily himself or prevent his daily chairing the risk-by-risk review. THAT IS HIS PRIORITY. Other activities, whether they be managerial tasks, market responsibilities or whatever, must be regarded as of secondary priority and cancelled if they interfere with his underwriting and control of his deputies' underwriting.

F. THE TEAM

An underwriting organisation must be a team, and it must be managed.

As our business develops we will need underwriters for different aspects of our business. For example,

Pro rata treaties
Third party and casualty excesses
Catastrophe and property excess
Marine and aviation
Facultative

or by area, for example:
USA and elsewhere.

If we haven't in-house experience we may have to import talent but it must be done carefully so as not to upset the team.

The underwriter in charge of a particular part of the account must be set clear objectives, as to both profitability and volume. Better still, he should set these himself in conjunction with the underwriting team, the team being the boss plus the departmental underwriters. In setting these objectives (at least annually) they will take into account general business factors, market competition, and prospects for profit, the object being to develop areas with potential profit and cut back where profit is not anticipated.

This process of forward planning is, of course, the prime duty of the chief underwriter, but it is vital that in reaching decisions he works with and through his departmental underwriters so that a team philosophy emerges.

This development of an underwriting team, and its involvement in planning and execution, should mean that a well-run underwriting insurance operation should never have to bring in top underwriters from outside. If this is necessary it is a failure of management.

Management should always ensure sufficient strength within the team to be able to promote naturally from within and to do this management must know its team, not just appoint a prima donna underwriter. It must make sure the team functions properly and recruits and trains young people all the time.

Finally, the underwriting team is the prime team of an insurance operation; it must never be dominated by the investment team or the accountancy team or the computer. These ancillary services are there to provide a service to the underwriters; they must never become their masters.

G. INTEGRITY

Our future, and that of our company, will depend, in the long term, on the trust our clients place in us. Your word, and the word of any member of your staff, is your bond. Verbal agreements are contracts (but do record them). No action of ours should damage this integrity and trust and, once established, it is our most precious asset.

Similarly, select your clients from people you can trust. Some reassureds regard reinsurance as something to be taken advantage of, i.e. to be exploited.

They expect to make a profit out of their reinsurers to enhance their own doubtful net results. "There is always another mug when we've burnt up this one."

Others genuinely treat their reinsurers as partners in a joint venture. They expect reinsurers to make a profit for the service they provide. Eschew the former and cultivate the latter.

Treat your reinsurers in the way you would want to be treated yourself.

Why me?

Never forget that reinsurance is not a friendly pool of nice friendly fish. It is an unfriendly sea full of sharks and piranhas and Portuguese Men of War and a few other nationalities too!

Some people may like you, others may trust you and want you to see and underwrite their good business. Before ever setting pen to paper ask yourself "why me?".

Why is this person asking *me* to underwrite this piece of business? And if you do not know the answer or if the answer is flattering to you, stop, think and reconsider.

Be aware of the following:

(1) Lots of orders on your quotations (you are too cheap).
(2) Long queues to see you (you are writing too freely).
(3) Market chatter reported from friends about your progress.
(4) Other underwriters' comments, and are the slips you write well supported by other sensible underwriters?

Innocence

Innocence is no excuse! Never underwrite something you do not fully understand. Never agree to initial something you do not understand. Never worry about asking questions, never worry about being considered ignorant or foolish. Much better to admit your ignorance before accepting the business. In most cases everyone else will be ignorant too.

Backing your team

You, as the boss, and each member of your team must support each other. You back each other's decisions in public, you never correct a junior in front of a client or broker. You must never publicly override your juniors. If you feel they have made an underwriting error, tell them so in private and let them correct it with the client or broker.

H. CONSTRUCTIVE UNDERWRITING

It is easy in difficult times to write no new business and maybe that can be better than writing too freely but the good underwriter should always, if possible, make terms. "I would accept that treaty if ceding commission were 22.5% not 27.5%" or "Surely, instead of a treaty on your hail account, you ought to think of a stop loss excess of, say, 90% loss ratio. It would work like this and my cost would be so much".

The job of a reinsurer is to help the insurer and constructive advice is one way of doing this.

Now the scenes are set, we have planned our action. Let the curtain rise!

I. DISPUTES (1989 NOTE)

My experience during the last few years as an arbitrator, expert witness or consultant in some 70 disputes in the reinsurance field has been an eye opener. The disputes have involved a total of several billion dollars in total, nearly all of them arising out of bad faith by one or all parties, allied to sheer greed or stupidity. For example, by reassureds and their brokers deliberately misleading their reinsurers by "clever wordings" or by non-disclosure or veiled non-disclosure. Reinsurers not even reading slips or, if they have, not understanding them and producing no wordings and not asking questions.

The courts in the UK (but not in the USA) have come down strongly in favour of requiring disclosure of any information that would influence a prudent reinsurer. They have placed less stress on the duty of the reinsurer to ask questions.

There are two views on most of these disputes. One is that some reassureds, and in particular placing brokers, have deliberately and consistently taken innocent reinsurers for a ride. The second view is that reinsurers have imprudently taken on contracts and, having deliberately done so, are now ratting on those contracts, often years later, for any reason they think will delay payment and force a compromise, or even a verdict, in their favour.

Good faith and integrity, if it ever existed, has long gone out of the window. In my view both views have validity and both are equally common.

Whatever the outcome of the courts or arbitration, it is expensive and subject to long delays.

My advice in this chapter is more valid than ever. If you are writing business, read the slip and information, understand it, record it, double check it, ask "why me?" and do not trust every broker too far. ASK QUESTIONS and record the answers.

If you are the reassured, disclose fully and check that your broker has done so. Act in good faith and do not accept a quote that you yourself know to be ridiculously cheap or unsound, because if you place a reinsurance by taking advantage of a stupid reinsurer it will bring you trouble and rightly so. Choose your placing broker for his integrity not his cleverness and choose your reinsurers from stable people who know what they are doing, not the latest "pen happy" idiot in the Market.

CHAPTER 6

UNDERWRITING EXAMPLES 1983–1985

The following examples are taken from actual slips provided from the London and International Market. They are, of course, anonymous and certain details have been modified to preserve that anonymity as best I can. I am grateful to several friends for providing them.

The information provided in most cases was voluminous; for some propositions the information ran into many pages. I have extracted and summarised the essential information partly for the sake of brevity and also as I believe this is in itself a very valuable exercise in the analysis of a proposition. I would suggest that any underwriter should do this automatically in considering any complicated reinsurance proposition. I find the actual work of writing down the essential details clarifies one's thoughts.

I have deliberately kept my analysis brief and simple. No two people will underwrite in the same way and I am not suggesting that my answers are correct. I am suggesting to the reader only the type of process that he himself should carry out.

I have included a checklist or summary of some of the relevant points to be taken into account of each type of reinsurance.

I would suggest that with each case the reader reads the slip briefly, then the information, then re-reads the information and relates it to the slip. Then re-read the slip in detail line by line and word by word so that all of its nuances are fully understood, with notes being made of any unusual features and the most important factors. Then make up your own mind as to the proposition's merits or demerits and decide whether you would write it or not and why, and the line you would accept.

Then see if you and I agree; actually, whether we agree or not is not important. What is important is for you to develop your own ability to assess each risk according to your own underwriting objectives.

AIDES-MEMOIRE TO UNDERWRITING ASSESSMENT

(a) Treaties

Financial considerations: to arrive at the extent, if any, of the cash and financial gain or penalty

> Currency problem and remittance problems
> Companies' financial strength
> Earned or written income
> Premium reserve
> Loss reserve
> Interest thereon
> Payment of amounts owing
> Size of cash loss payments for claims

General: the general results and prospects of the areas of business

> The company's specific prospects and quality of its underwriters
> Past results and trends on an earned incurred basis
> Adequacy of the outstanding loss reserving
> Acquisition cost *vis-à-vis* commission
> Effect of profit commission and sliding scale
> Perils covered and catastrophic exposures
> PML and risk exposures
> Anticipated profit margins to cover risk and catastrophic exposures
> Any changes of underwriting policy and personnel
> Extra charges, brokerage, tax, etc.
> Adequacy of any incoming loss reserve
> Double check if any long-tail exposure.

(b) Catastrophe excesses

> Management of catastrophe exposures
> Past losses—their likely cost next year on current business
> Their likely recurrence
> Exposures by peril, by area, likely loss to layer and probability of such loss
> Any per risk exposure
> Future and past underwriting changes, i.e. new areas
> Rate on line
> Have you spare capacity?
> Line limits—are these pro rata reinsured or first loss retentions?
> Original deductibles.

(c) Risk excesses

Risk attaching or losses occurring basis
Past record on present line limits
Present income with inflation adjustment
Is there free cover?
Occurrence limit and catastrophic exposure
Exposed values or exposed value premium income
Future underwriting and rating
Any first loss or excess loss business written
Class of business, e.g. petrochemicals.

(d) Third party, workmen's compensation, motor

Quality of claims management
Laws relating to awards
Policy limits
Level of court awards per person
Legal expenses
Rate of likely inflation of awards
Past record indexed
IBNR estimate
Triangulation of past results
Hazardous classes and catastrophic potential
Industrial and latent disease
Retrospective awards. Court attitudes
Products, pollution risks
Environmental risk
Aggregate exposures
USA exposures.

(e) Stop loss

If long-tail—decline
General trends in experience in class
Companies' prospects and reason for purchasing stop loss
Past statistics; are these viable on present underwriting, e.g. rates the same, exposure and lines the same?
Future underwriting line limits, classes and rate changes
Exposures to catastrophic risks
Basis of figures earned/incurred?
Adequacy of outstanding loss reserves
Check that figures are on identical basis as contract. All deductions the same

Reinsurance cost deducted and past reinsurance maintained
Will reassured lose money at suggested deductible and premium?
How much?
Does premium relate to *future* loss exposure and frequency?
Is it fair?
Compare to quota share terms, i.e. unlimited
Stop loss excess of 70% loss ratio for 5% equals quota share with commission 25% 100% profit commission with 5% expenses
Is fortuity involved or are we protecting just poor underwriting?

(f) Facultative

Quality of insured
Coverage and perils, rates, i.e. would you write the original business?
Record
Commission asked in relation to reassured cost. Override tax and brokerage?
How much do you trust reassured's judgement?
What is he keeping *net*?
Economics of premium and your line.

In general, these underwriting assessment processes can be taken in stages:

(a) Evaluation of the country or areas and general results prospect on an industry or class basis. The political and economic risks.
(b) The evaluation of the company, its reputation, records and of course, its owners, managers, underwriters.
(c) The evaluation of the projects of the actual proposition making an underwriting or technical profit for you and how much.
(d) The evaluation of the cash flow and investment profit it will bring in or reverse.
(e) (c) + (d) = prospect of an overall profit.
(f) If (e) is sufficiently positive for you the assessment of line on your estimate of the likely maximum loss to you.

PROPOSITION 1

SLIP DETAILS

REASSURED: A major USA insurance company.

PERIOD: Continuation as from 1 January 1985 on continuous treaty from 1 January 1968, subject to 90 days' notice of cancellation to any anniversary.
It is agreed that in the event of termination of the above treaty, the company have the following options:
1. Continue liability in force to not longer than first anniversary date of termination of treaty and reinsurers liable for outstanding losses with no loss portfolio.
2. Relieve reinsurers of all liability at date of termination and reinsurers liable for outstanding losses, with no loss portfolio.

TYPE: OBLIGATORY FIRST SURPLUS.

CLASS: Covering fire and allied lines, inland marine and multi-peril business, including homeowners and similar forms of writings on manufacturers' output policies and automobile physical damage business.

TREATY DETAIL: To take cessions any one risk up to US$15,000,000 probable maximum loss any one risk subject to a limit of US$30,000,000 any one risk but not exceeding five retentions. Minimum retention US$250,000 any one risk.
Retention subject to excess loss reinsurance.

RATE: Gross original rate.

COMMISSION: 27.5% provisional commission subject to a minimum commission of 25% at 70% loss ratio, then increasing by 1% for each one percent (1%) reduction in loss ratio to 30% commission at 65% loss ratio, then increasing by half percent (.5%) for each one percent (1%) reduction in loss ratio to a maximum commission of 40% at 45% loss ratio.

	Debit/credit carried forward (three-year limitation). Sliding scale being calculated provisionally at close of each annual period and finally adjusted 12 months after close of each annual period.
TAXES:	1% Federal Excise Tax (where applicable).
BROKERAGE:	2% on gross.
PREMIUM RESERVE:	Premiums accounted on an earned premium basis.
LOSS RESERVE:	LOC but cash OCA for Canadian dollars as required by reassured (non-admitted reinsurers only).
CASH LOSS:	US$250,000.
ACCOUNTS:	Monthly accounts with quarterly settlement. Earned premium basis.
GENERAL CONDITIONS:	Pools and associations exclusion clause. War exclusion clause. R/I tax clause. Nuclear incident exclusion clauses—liability and physical damage—reinsurance. TIV exclusion clause ($200,000,000—as per wording). New intermediary clause. Insolvency funds exclusion clause.
WORDING:	Wording and exclusions as before or as may be agreed by leading non-marine underwriter.

INFORMATION

Company well-known writer of all lines in all states.

The business ceded to the treaty is mainly industrial and commercial property business nationwide.

The company's acquisition costs are:

    18.0% Average commission to agents
    2.5% State fees and taxes
    4.0% Engineering fees

Results

	GEPI	Paid	O/S	Incurred	Losses (US$000) LR
1979	20,000	12,000	Nil	12,000	60%
1980	25,000	16,500	1,000	17,500	70%
1981	30,000	21,600	Nil	21,600	72%
1982	32,000	24,000	1,600	25,600	80%
1983	33,000	23,000	2,100	25,100	76%
1984 (to 30/6)	17,000	4,000	8,200	12,200	72%

The largest individual loss was US$4,500,000 in 1982.

The company has reviewed its rating and selection of business since 1981 with greater selection, elimination of poor agents and reduction in rating discounts. It is confident that its policies will improve results for 1984 and 1985. It intends to increase its writing for 1985 selectively to around US$40,000,000.

ASSESSMENT

First, one must assess the general prospects for US commercial and industrial business for 1985 and 1986. 1983 and 1984 results have been terrible. However, there are signs that some remedial action has been taken and 1985 and 1986 could show some improvement. Therefore, selective underwriting of better treaties might make sense.

Turning to this treaty it has a large PML and risk limit in relation to the income. Experience has been steady, and not unreasonable, through a bad period and shows a slight improvement for 1983 and possibly for 1984.

The sliding scale will have deficits coming in from 1982, 1983 and 1984 and the 1985 ceding commission is likely to be held at 25%. If this proves correct then with the provisional commission at 27.5% not much financing (2.5%) is involved.

On an earned basis there will be only a small premium balance for investment.

On balance a fair write with prospects of a reasonable profit if recovery continues. However, a large PML and risk exposure.

		US$
Line risk limit	30,000,000	
Maximum line 1%	300,000 per risk	
PML	150,000	

For a gross income of US$400,000.

Possible loss ratio 68% and commission 25% to give a gross profit of 7% less brokerage of 2% which is 5% net or US$20,000.

1995 comment

None.

PROPOSITION 2

SLIP DETAILS

REASSURED:	A German insurance company.
PERIOD:	To attach 1 January 1984 continuous subject to three months' notice of cancellation to expire at 31 December any one year.
TYPE:	FIRST SURPLUS FIRE TREATY.
CLASS:	To cover fire, lightning, explosion and consequential loss following fire as underwritten by the ceding company.
TERRITORIAL SCOPE:	Federal Republic of Germany, West Berlin and German interests abroad.
TREATY DETAIL:	To take hereunder nine-times the ceding company's retention of DM500,000 PML but maximum PML cession hereunder not exceeding DM4,500,000.
COMMISSION:	20% plus fire tax 5%.
BROKERAGE:	2.5%.
PREMIUM RESERVE:	40%. Interest: 6%.
CLAIMS PORTFOLIO:	90%—on termination portfolio may be allowed to run off.
PREMIUM PORTFOLIO:	35%—on termination portfolio may be allowed to run off.
CASH LOSS:	DM100,000 for 100%.
ACCOUNTS:	Quarterly.
GENERAL CONDITIONS:	Premium calculation clause. Target risks clause (*Spitzenrisken*). PML wrong estimation clause—contractual limitation of reinsurers liability of PML. Loss participation clause—from 78.5% LR. 20% participation (limit 8%).
WORDING:	Contract wording as expiring or as co-reinsurers or as agreed by leading reinsurer.

INFORMATION

Estimated premium income 1984: DM9,000,000

Results

DM

	Gross earned premiums	Incurred losses	LR
1978	12,000,000	6,000,000	50%
1979	12,000,000	12,000,000	100%
1980	13,000,000	19,000,000	146%
1982	14,000,000	14,000,000	100%
1983	As at 30.9.83. The earned ratio is 50% on a volume, rather less than 1982.		

The company are making the following changes to the treaty for 1984:

(1) Reducing capacity from 15 lines to 9 lines and maximum from DM7,500,000 to DM4,500,000.
(2) Reducing ceding commission to 20%.
(3) Doubling net retentions on all industrial risks.
(4) Increasing interest on reserves to 6%.

It is not known what improvement this would have made on past results.

ASSESSMENT

In many ways one would prefer to wait a year to see whether this one will improve. There are no signs at end of 1983 of any overall improvement in German business for 1984. These results are terrible. Logically, this proposition must be declined. However, if one has faith in German business the terms are right. There are signs of a possible improvement in 1982 and 1983.

The company is a first-class, old-established, direct insurer and the treaty is led by a good German reinsurer.

Emotionally, I am inclined to write a small line now as I feel that in 1984 or 1985 this will improve.

Maximum PML exposure DM4,500,000 or US$1,250,000.

The annual loss ratio could easily be 170% which would mean a loss of 90% of DM10,000,000 or DM9,000,000, giving a PML to the treaty of $2,500,000.

A 2.5% line equals an exposure of US$62,500 for an income of the same amount (gross).

NB Please note the two special clauses both often found in the German market:

(1) The contractual limitation of reinsurers' liability to the PML.
(2) The take back by the ceding company of a co-reinsurance of losses exceeding a 78.5% loss ratio.

1995 comment

None.

PROPOSITION 3A

SLIP DETAILS

REASSURED:	A Philippine insurance company.
PERIOD:	Continuous contract commencing 1 January 1984 subject to three months' notice of cancellation to any 31 December.
TYPE:	FIRST SURPLUS FIRE TREATY.
TERRITORIAL SCOPE:	Philippines.
TYPE OF BUSINESS:	Fire and allied perils written in the fire department of the reassured.
LIMIT:	Five lines not exceeding Pesos 7,500,000.
COMMISSION:	37.5% PLUS 2.5% if loss ratio is 35% or less.
PROFIT COMMISSION:	30%. Reinsurer's expenses 5%. Three-year average.
PREMIUM RESERVE:	40% gross. Interest 5%.
BROKERAGE:	2.5%.
PREMIUM TAX:	4%.
PREMIUM PORTFOLIO:	35%.
OUTSTANDING LOSSES:	90%.
CASH LOSS:	Pesos 500,000 (100% of treaty).
BORDEREAUX:	Nil.
ACCOUNTS:	Quarterly.
WORDING:	To be agreed (leading underwriter only).

INFORMATION

Estimated premium: Pesos 40 million.

First surplus results

Pesos

	Earned premiums	Incurred losses	Earned incurred LR
1976	13,000,000	3,800,000	29%
1977	15,000,000	6,200,000	41%
1978	16,600,000	17,600,000	106%
1979	19,200,000	23,000,000	120%
1980	20,800,000	11,500,000	55%
1981	24,400,000	19,000,000	78%
1982	27,500,000	30,200,000	110%
1983	15,000,000	10,000,000	66%

Outstanding losses at 30 June 1983—Pesos 27,000,000 for year 1980 to 1983 included in the incurred figures.

PROPOSITION 3B

SLIP DETAILS

REASSURED: A Philippine insurance company.

PERIOD: Continuous contract commencing 1 January 1984 subject to three months' notice of cancellation to any 31 December.

TYPE: SECOND SURPLUS FIRE TREATY.

TERRITORIAL SCOPE: Philippines.

TYPE OF BUSINESS: Fire and allied perils written in the fire department of the reassured.

LIMIT: Five lines not exceeding Pesos 7,500,000.

COMMISSION: 35% plus 2.5% if loss ratio is 35% or less.

PROFIT COMMISSION: 30%. Reinsurer's expenses 5%. Three-year average.

PREMIUM RESERVE: 40%. Interest 5%.

BROKERAGE: 2.5%.

PREMIUM TAX: 4%.

PORTFOLIO: (Entry/Withdrawal).

PREMIUM: 35%.

OUTSTANDING LOSSES: 90%.

CASH LOSS LIMIT: Pesos 150,000 (100% of treaty).

BORDEREAUX: Nil.

ACCOUNTS: Quarterly.

WORDING: To be agreed (leading underwriter only).

INFORMATION

Estimated premium income 1985 (100%) Pesos 14,000,000.

Second surplus results

Pesos

	Gross written	Gross earned	Losses incurred	Earned LR
1976	4,000,000	3,800,000	760,000	20%
1977	4,800,000	4,500,000	1,125,000	25%
1978	6,000,000	5,500,000	5,000,000	91%
1979	6,500,000	6,200,000	4,960,000	80%
1980	7,000,000	6,800,000	3,750,000	55%
1981	9,000,000	8,200,000	7,400,000	90%
1982	10,000,000	9,600,000	13,400,000	140%
1983	11,000,000	10,600,000	5,800,000	55%

PROPOSITIONS 3A AND 3B

GENERAL ASSESSMENT

The Philippines' political situation is difficult with possible unrest and arson. Fire results are poor and prospects uncertain. We may also have remittance problems.

Turning to these treaties: on the First Surplus the total outgoings are 37.5% plus 2.5% plus 4% = 44% in all. Therefore there will be no profit unless loss ratio is under 55% and that has not been achieved since 1976 and 1977. In addition, a premium reserve of 40% of the gross, plus costs of 44%, leaves us with only 16% to pay all the losses. Interest on the reserve is only 5%.

Conclusion

The possibility of long-term profit is remote.

On the Second Surplus we have a total outgoing of 35% plus 4% plus 2.5% = 41.5% and the same conclusion is reached.

This company's first and second surplus treaties are both hopeless underwriting propositions as offered. Therefore we should decline them.

If it is possible to negotiate then a lot of information is needed, e.g.:

— Earthquake and wind premium income.
— Earthquake exposures to each treaty by zone.
— Increases, if any, made in original rates.
— Congested block liabilities and lines.
— What steps have been taken or are to be taken over improving the direct underwriting?
— Who is the fire underwriter, how long has he been with the company and what is his past experience?

Whatever answers we get, and however favourable, they will not permit us to do better than the following:

First surplus

(a) Insert a minimum retention.
(b) Agree an exclusion list.
(c) Maximum commission around 25%, plus tax 4% and brokerage 2% = 31% in all.
(d) If premium reserve must be 40%, then interest should be 15% minimum.
(e) Cash loss limit Pesos 2,000,000.

Second surplus

As above, but total costs 27.5% in all.

As it may be most unlikely that the ceding company will, or can, accept our terms, as some mug will give them better, there is no point in wasting our time unless we get a "bite" at these terms or something near them.

PROPOSITION 4

SLIP DETAILS

REASSURED:	A US insurance company.
PERIOD:	Continuous contract from 12.01 a.m. 1 July, subject to four months' notice of cancellation to 30 June.
TYPE:	QUOTA SHARE TREATY.
CLASS:	Covering fire and allied lines, inland marine and multi-peril business including homeowners and similar forms of writings on manufacturers' output policies and automobile physical damage business.
TERRITORIAL SCOPE:	USA.
TREATY DETAIL:	27.5% quota share with limit hereon US$1,375,000 (being 27.5% of US$5,000,000).
RATE:	Gross original rate less a provisional commission of 27.50% adjustable for each calendar year as follows: — 20% minimum commission at 70% loss ratio increasing 2/3% for each 2% reduction in loss ratio to a maximum commission of 36-2/3% at 45% loss ratio debit carried forward. — Sliding scale to be provisionally computed at end of year and finally computed 12 months after close of year.
BROKERAGE:	Less 1% Federal Excise Tax (where applicable). 2.5% brokerage on gross.
LOSS RESERVE:	LOC (Citibank scheme) but cash OCA for Canadian dollars as required by reassured (non-admitted reinsurers only).
ACCOUNTS:	Quarterly.
GENERAL CONDITIONS:	War exclusion clause. Nuclear incident exclusion clause—physical damage—reinsurance. Tax clause (reinsurance). Insolvency funds exclusion clause. Intermediary clause.

Proposition 4

WORDING: Wording as before, as far as applicable, as agreed by leading underwriter.

INFORMATION

Best's report on the company is not impressive.

Company is writing a well-controlled account of medium-sized risks in Illinois and Mid-West with maximum lines per exposure as follows:

	US$	
Fire and allied	5,000,000	
Homeowners	500,000	
Inland marine and multi-peril	1,000,000	
Manufacturers' output	5,000,000	
Auto physical	1,000,000	a.o fleet

Original commissions average 17.5%.
Company started in 1974.

Statistics

			US$
	Gross premiums	Losses paid	Losses O/S
1980	2,500,000	1,750,000	Nil
1981	2,600,000	2,000,000	10,000
1982	3,500,000	2,200,000	50,000
1983	4,000,000	2,800,000	200,000
1984	4,000,000	1,000,000	800,000

The company filed a new rating schedule for much business in 1982 and intends to increase its volumes in 1985 to approximately US$6,000,000.

QUESTIONS

Q. Can we warrant that company keeps net the 72.5% for its own account? If not, what other reinsurer does it have and what is its net retention?

A. Company has additional quota share arrangements for 27.5%. Company keeps balance of 45% subject to excess of loss protection excess of US$100,000.

Q. May we warrant the line limits given in information and that any surplus over these limits is reinsured on a contributory basis or so deemed?

A. Yes, but company may reinsure larger risks on an excess basis according to exposure.

Q. Are the company writing first loss or excess insurance on any classes? If so, please give details of their underwriting policy?

A. In accordance with present market conditions they may write their exposure on the larger risks on this basis.

Q. Is treaty to be accounted on a written or earned basis?

A. Written, but before deduction of commissions.

Q. Are the figures given written or earned?

A. As above.

Q. Who is responsible for underwriting and what is their experience and record? Have they been conducting the underwriting since 1980?

A. The underwriting team changed in 1982. Since then it has been under the experienced control of Mr John Doe.

Q. Can we have the estimated breakdown of the 1984 premiums income by class of business?

A. Approximately—50% fire and allied
   20% homeowners
   20% auto
   10% inland marine and manufacturers' output.

ASSESSMENT

Results

US$000

	Gross written	Est. earned	Incurred losses	LR	Commission	Results
1981	2,600	2,600	2,010	77%	20%	+3%
1982	3,500	3,500	2,250	62.5%	25%	+12.5%
1983	4,000	4,000	3,000	75%	20%	+5%
1984	4,000	2,000	1,800	90%	20%	−10%

Less 2.5% brokerage.

Therefore, in a bad period, it is profitable at these low commission terms.

Account has obviously deteriorated since 1983. It is probably sub-standard business and includes first loss insurances and excess of loss insurances.

The company's net retention is very small indeed and we do not know how their net results will compare with ours.

Can we trust the outstanding loss estimates for 1983 and 1984?

I would only entertain this company if I knew much more about it and its financial position, its owners and if it kept a better net retention.

I think this could bring us trouble, so decline.

PROPOSITION 5

SLIP DETAILS

REASSURED:	A major Lloyd's Syndicate.
PERIOD:	Continuous cover always open for full amount in respect of business attaching to the 1984 underwriting account and subsequent underwriting accounts. Subject to three months' cancellation clause at end of any calendar year (not applying to risks already attached).
TYPE:	QUOTA SHARE TREATY.
INTEREST:	Confiscation and/or requisition and/or political risks as original including incidental war accounts and other accounts where the reassured is unable to separate the premium and in his view the risk is very substantially confiscation and/or requisition and/or political.
TREATY CONDITIONS:	Original conditions. Including war, strikes, riots and civil commotion risks when coverage is granted in conjunction with perils covered hereunder. To take a quota share of US$20,000,000 (50%) part of US$40,000,000 maximum gross limit per country and maximum gross limit of US$5,000,000 any one policy. Reassured to retain 50% (subject to excess of loss reinsurance).
WORDING:	Contract wording as expiring unless otherwise mutually agreed (with leading reinsurer).
LOSS RESERVE:	Letter of credit provision for outstanding claims, if required.
ACCOUNTS:	Quarterly.
CASH LOSS:	US$200,000 (or equivalent in other currencies).
COMMISSION:	10% + 5% brokerage.
PROFIT COMMISSION:	25% (subject to three years' deficit clause and 5% allowance for reinsurers' expenses).

INFORMATION

The syndicate is a leading syndicate at Lloyd's.

Statistics for 100%

US$

Year	Net premium subject to brokerage	Paid claims
1973	200,000	20,000
1974	700,000	120,000
1975	1,100,000	90,000
1976	1,200,000	40,000
1977	1,800,000	600,000
1978	1,400,000	750,000
1979	1,900,000	1,200,000
1980	1,900,000	600,000
1981	1,800,000	700,000
1982	2,200,000	200,000
1983	400,000	50,000
	14,600,000	4,370,000

Outstanding claims

- 1981 US$400,000
- 1982 US$600,000
- 1983 Three possible for total of US$700,000

NB 1983 Premium expected to be around US$2,000,000
1984 US$3,000,000 anticipated.

ASSESSMENT

A pure quota share of a good syndicate in an unusual "London" type of business.

The 10% overrider is not unfair and profit commission heavy but not excessive. It is obviously unbalanced with a 100% limit of US$5,000,000 a policy and US$40,000,000 per country against an income of US$3,000,000.

The record is good and taking a quota share of an acknowledged expert on such business may be a lot more economic than writing this class ourselves. So let us have a line of, say, 1.5% of 50% quota share for a line of US$37,500 per contract, US$300,000 per country and an income of US$22,500, then we will not write additional lines elsewhere.

1995 comment

This was a mistake for these reasons. It was not a quota share but was used only to cede heavier risks. The expert proved to be the opposite and the reassured did not keep 50%.

We repudiated liability and made a compromise settlement.

PROPOSITION 6

SLIP DETAILS

REASSURED:	A UK company.
PERIOD:	Losses occurring during the period 12 months commencing 1 January 1984.
TYPE:	FIRST FIRE CATASTROPHE HOME AND OVERSEAS EXCESS OF LOSS REINSURANCE.
CLASS:	(1) The reinsured's net retained account of direct insurance and facultative reinsurances in respect of: (a) Home and overseas business written in its fire departments and certain proportional treaty arrangements written in the overseas fire department. (b) Its participation in the business of international oil insurers written in its fire departments. (2) Fire and allied perils written in the home personal department in respect of the reinsured's householders' comprehensive and private dwelling house policies including small craft and caravans.
TERRITORIAL SCOPE:	Worldwide, excluding risks situated in the USA, but this exclusion shall not apply to risks where the operation insured by the reinsured is multinational and the portion situated within the USA forms an integral part of the whole. It is understood that exposures in the USA form a minor part of the reinsured's total portfolio hereunder.
LIMIT:	£2,250,000 ultimate net loss each and every loss occurrence in excess of £750,000 ultimate net loss each and every loss occurrence. For freeze extension clause, additional deductible of £250,000.
REINSTATEMENT:	One full reinstatement at 100% additional premium as to time, pro rata as to amount reinstated only.
PREMIUM:	Rate: 1.25% of gross net premium income. Minimum and deposit: £400,000 payable half yearly in advance.

DEDUCTIONS:	Brokerage 10% (nil on reinstatement premium).
GENERAL CONDITIONS:	Ultimate net loss. Net retained lines. War and civil war exclusion. Nuclear energy and atomic exclusion to be agreed (leading underwriter only). Excess of loss treaty reinsurance exclusion. Currency fluctuation clause (as attached). Definition of loss occurrence (as attached).

CURRENCY FLUCTUATION CLAUSE

(1) In the event that the reinsured sustains losses in a currency other than sterling, the reinsurers' liability shall be calculated as follows:

  (i) The underlying losses, and the limit of indemnity as expressed in sterling in items 5, 6 and 7 of the schedule, shall be converted into currency concerned at the rates of exchange utilised by the reinsured in its books at the commencement date of this agreement

  (ii) the balance of any loss payment in excess of the underlying losses shall be converted from the currency in which the loss was settled into sterling at the rate of exchange as used by the reinsured and ruling on the date or dates of settlement of the loss by the reinsured.

(2) In the event that losses are sustained by the reinsured in respect of the same loss occurrence in more than one currency, the underlying losses, and the limit of indemnity, shall be apportioned between the various currencies in the proportion that each currency bears to the total loss calculated by converting each currency into sterling at the rate of exchange as indicated in paragraph (1). The balance of any loss payment in each original currency, in excess of the underlying losses in each currency apportioned as above, shall be converted into sterling at the rate of exchange used by the reinsured and ruling on the date or dates of settlement of the loss by the reinsured.

DEFINITION OF LOSS OCCURRENCE

The words "loss occurrence" shall mean all individual losses arising out of, and directly occasioned by, one catastrophe. However, the duration and extent of any "loss occurrence" so defined shall be limited to:

(a) 72 consecutive hours as regards hurricane, typhoon, windstorm, rainstorm, hailstorm and/or tornado;
(b) 72 consecutive hours as regards earthquake, seaquake, tidal wave and/or volcanic eruption;
(c) 72 consecutive hours and within the limits of one country as regards riots, civil commotions and malicious damage;
(d) 72 consecutive hours as regards any "loss occurrence" which includes individual loss or losses from any of the perils mentioned in (a), (b) and (c) above;
(e) 168 consecutive hours for any "loss occurrence" of whatsoever nature which does not include individual loss or losses from any of the perils mentioned in (a), (b) and (c) above;

and no individual loss from whatever peril, which occurs outside these periods or areas, shall be included in that "loss occurrence".

The reinsured may choose the date and time when any such period of consecutive hours commences and, if any catastrophe is of greater duration than the above periods, the reinsured may divide that catastrophe into two or more "loss occurrences", provided no two periods overlap and provided no period commences earlier than the date and time of the happening of the first recorded individual loss to the reinsured in that catastrophe.

Notwithstanding the above, as regards loss or losses from collapse caused by weight of snow and water damage from burst pipes and/or melting snow, the reinsured shall have the option to deem any one "loss occurrence" to be the aggregate of all such individual losses which occur during a period of 168 consecutive hours within one continent. No period may commence earlier than the date and time of the happening of the first recorded individual loss to the reinsured in that "loss occurrence" and the period of two or more "loss occurrences" may not overlap. It is understood and agreed, however, that if the reinsured exercises the option set out in this paragraph, then the amount in excess of which this agreement attaches shall be increased for the "loss occurrence" or "loss occurrences" involved by the amount of £250,000.

Second layer as first layer
but £2,000,000 excess of £3,000,000
Min. & Dep. £72,500
Rate .2% gnpi–10%

Third layer £5,000,000 excess of £5,000,000
Min. & Dep. £110,000
Rate .325%–10%

Fourth layer £10,00,000 excess of £10,000,000
Min. & Dep. £140,000
Rate .375%–10%

Proposition 6

Third and fourth total loss on first layer	£2,250,000 excess of £750,000 e.e. loss but only to pay when the first catastrophe layer is fully exhausted by payment of £4,500,000 of losses Premium £70,000 Reinstatements—one at 100% AP.

INFORMATION

£000

	Premium income	Losses from ground up over £400,000	
1976	18,000	1,800	
1977	20,000	600	
1978	21,000	800	SW floods (UK)
1979	25,000	1,300	Heavy weather
1980	30,000	(Nil)	
1981	35,000	1,100	Winter weather UK
1982	38,000	2,000	Bad weather UK
		1,700	Bad weather UK
1982	40,000	Nil	

£000

Income breakdown 1983:	UK fire Householders Overseas	15,000 19,000 6,000
Estimated 1984 premium income:		42,000
Maximum limits:	Class 1 risk	500 EML plus 50% for loss of profits
Previous large losses:	Flixborough 1974 European storms 1976 Storms 1978	500 1,800 600
Earthquake liabilities:	Israel Abu Dhabi Saudi Arabia Others under	50,000 26,000 25,000 20,000
Windstorm:	Bahamas Trinidad Jamaica Others under	24,000 8,000 5,000 5,000

Included in overseas income and liabilities is the company's share in international oil insurers pool of £500,000 EML income approximately £390,000.

SUMMARY AND ASSESSMENT

A medium-large UK company with nearly 50% of its business from UK homeowners and small business and, as losses show, exposed to UK winter weather and storms.

First layer

£2,250,000 excess of £750,000 earns 1.25% times £42,000,000 = £525,000 for rate on line of 23%. With reinstatement at 100% for time a total loss at any time will produce an AP of £525,000 making effective rate on line nearly 30% for the first loss.

Loss record indexed up to PI of £42,000,000.

		Loss record
		Loss hereon
1976 Storm of £1.8m ×	$\frac{42}{19}$ = £4,000,000	£2,250,000
1978 Storm of £0.6m ×	$\frac{42}{25}$ = £1,200,000	£450,000
1979 Floods of £0.8m ×	$\frac{42}{25}$ = £1,350,000	£600,000
1979 Heavy weather of £1.13m ×	$\frac{42}{25}$ = £2,100,000	£1,360,000
1981 Winter of £1.1m ×	$\frac{42}{35}$ = £1,370,000	£370,000
NB Deductible £1,000,000		
1982(1) Bad weather £2m ×	$\frac{42}{38}$ = £2,210,000	£1,210,000
NB Deductible £1,000,000		
1982(2) Bad weather £1.7m ×	$\frac{42}{38}$ = £1,870,000	£870,000
NB Deductible £1,000,000		
	Total	£7,110,000

On "as if" basis therefore over 10 years one would have paid out £7,110,000 against an annual premium of £525,000 plus some reinstatement APs, i.e. £5,250,000 plus reinstatement APs of approximately £1,720,000 for a 10 year premium of £7,000,000.

Other factors

The deductible is excess of the maximum EML exposure but some residual risk exposure may be there. Also no overseas loss, except the 1976 European storm, is included and thus this cover is granted free.

Clearly this first layer is seriously underrated and we will decline it.

If the policy was for £2,000,000 excess of £1,000,000 at 1.25%, the £7,100,000 "as if" losses would be reduced to £5,350,000 which, although below cost, might be worth a flutter at a rate on line of 26% plus reinstatement.

Second layer

			"As If" record
			Loss hereon
1976	Storm	£4,000,000	£1,000,000
1979		£2,110,000	Nil
1982		£2,210,000	Nil
		£1,870,000	

Premium .2 × £42,000,000 = £84,000

Rate on line 4.2%

One should note that the 1982 losses approach the deductible, and the combined weather loss would be over £4,000,000. Even ignoring other worldwide exposures a sizeable loss to this layer must be probable, at least in every 10 years, and this layer is rated too low.

To attract me the rate on line should be around 7% to 8% for a rate of .35% = £147,000. Therefore decline.

Third layer

1976 Loss £4,000,000
1982 Combined £4,080,000 } No losses hereon

Layer £5m excess of £5m for rate .325% = £136,500.
Rate on line 2.72%.

Fourth layer

£10m excess of £10m for rate .375% = £157,500.
Rate on line 1.575%.

On both these layers the loss experience is nil. On neither layer is there any single risk exposure.

The exposures worldwide for earthquake excess of £10m are negligible, except for Israel, and even there, very remote.

The windstorm in the Caribbean is likewise most remote excess of £10m and excess of £5m it is not serious.

The UK/European exposure excess of £5m is there with a UK homeowners income of £19m but excess of £10m must be remote.

Bearing in mind the assessments of future probabilities:

    Layer 2 £2m excess of £3m   at 4.2%   rate on line
    Layer 3 £5m excess of £5m   at 2.72%   rate on line
    Layer 4 £10m excess of £10m at 1.75%   rate on line

There is no doubt in my mind that Layer 3 is better than Layer 2 and Layer 4 is better than Layer 3. Therefore, we should write Layer 4 and in my view the chance of a £10m loss must be of the order of 50:1 against and a £20m loss greater than that.

I would regard Layer 4 as suitable for maximum commitment, plus a treaty cession.

Say, 2.5% for £250,000 or 7.5% with our treaty.

First layer, third and fourth loss

£2,250,000 each and every loss excess of £750,000 each and every loss excess of £4,500,000 in aggregate. £4,500,000 in all.

Premium £70,000.

1982—Aggregate losses to first layer, £2,080,000 for two bad weather losses. Had the year suffered a third, say, storm loss like 1976, it would have added £2,250,000. Still no involvement.

The first layer earns	£525,000 for first loss
plus (reinstatement premiums)	£121,000 for second loss
Premium hereon is	£70,000 for third loss

Although the £525,000 and £121,000 are too low, the £70,000 premium does not look unreasonable. It produces a rate on line of just over 3%. It rates better than the third layer and not far off the 4.2% rate on line on the second layer.

I think a small line of 2% net 6% with our treaty would be a fair chance.

1995 note

I think my decision was correct, but the UK hurricane 87J in 1987 may have wrecked even layer 4, and 1989 more so.

PROPOSITION 7

SLIP DETAILS

REASSURED: A USA Mid-West mutual.

PERIOD: Continuation from 1 January 1984 on continuous contract from 1 January 1981 subject to 90 days' notice of cancellation at 31 December of any year. To cover losses occurring during the period of the contract.

TYPE: FIRST PER RISK EXCESS OF LOSS COVER.

CLASS: Property business.

TERRITORIAL SCOPE: As original policies.

LIMIT: To pay the excess of US$500,000 each risk.
Limit hereunder US$500,000 each risk.
Subject to a limit of US$1,500,000 ultimate net loss any one occurrence.

PREMIUM: Rate 1% on gross net earned premium income.
Annual minimum premium US$475,000.
Annual deposit premium US$507,000 payable one fourth quarterly in advance.

DEDUCTIONS: Less 15% and 1% Federal Excise Tax as applicable.

INFORMATION

The company is a well-reputed and substantial mutual company in the Mid-West of the United States.

Earned premium income

    1983   US$60,000,000
    1984   US$65,000,000

Property limit profile

By percentage of premium income

    500,000– 750,000   2%

750,000–1,000,000   2%
1,000,000–1,500,000 2%
1,500,000–2,000,000 1%

This is a limit profile not based on a PML or EML.

Other blanket policies, mainly blanket school policies, over many locations—5%.

The company do not write first loss and do not write excess insurance.

Main state breakdown

Over US$1,500,000 premium income
Illinois	2,100,000
Iowa	5,000,000
N. Carolina	1,600,000
Mississippi	1,500,000
N. Dakota	1,500,000
Texas	1,500,000

Losses

To layer 500,000 × 500,000

1977	500,000 TL
	140,000
1978	100,000
1979	210,000
	250,000
1980	Nil
1981	450,000
1982	200,000
1983	250,000 o/s

1982 Rate 1.15%
1983 Rate 1.10%
1984 Rate 1%

Rate reduced due to record and exposure reductions.

ASSESSMENT

The premium income for earlier years is not given but if we assumed:

	Income Million	Losses	
1977	35	640,000	
1978	40	100,000	
1979	40	460,000	
1980	45	Nil	
1981	50	450,000	
1982	55	200,000	
1983	60	250,000	o/s
Total	325	2,100,000	
5 years	250	1,360,000	

7 years BC = .64% loaded 100/66% = .95%

US$

No free cover as at least one Total Loss.
Over five years, 1979–83, inclusive BC .524 × 100/66% = .79%
NB Here we use a loading of 100/66% as the brokerage is 15% not 10%.
Percentage of ground up premium calculated on the risks exposed (in US$):

    (a) 500,000 to 750,000 limit.
        Average exposure say 100,000 excess of 500,000—i.e. 16% excess of 83% worth, say 4%, of the premium for risk exposed.
    (b) 750,000, to 1,000,000 limit.
        Average exposure say 400,000 excess of 500,000—i.e. 44% excess of 56% worth say 18% of risk exposed premium.
    (c) 1,000,000 to 1,500,000 limit.
        Average exposure say 1,250,000—i.e. 40% excess of 40%, worth say, 22% of risk exposed premium.
    (d) 1,500,000 to 2,000,000 limit.
        Average risk exposure say 1,750,000—i.e. 30% excess of 30%, worth say 30%.

Thus

    (a) 4% × 2% = .08
    (b) 18% × 2% = .36
    (c) 22% × 2% = .44
    (d) 30% × 1% = .30

       Total   1.18

      plus something extra for schedules, say, .12 extra

        Total 1.30%
        less commission
        cost, say, 25% .325%

Net rate
on exposures 0.975%

Of these two calculations the BC over seven years produces a rate of .95%. Over five years produces a rate of .79%.

The profile on exposures a rate of .975%.

Of these the profile calculation is the most important.

It may be significant that the experience has not worsened due to inflation and it would appear that the company is conservative with its limits. It is significant that the profile is on a sum insured basis with no first loss or excess loss policies.

The rate appears reasonable and will produce US$650,000 gross − 15% = US$563,000 which will pay a TL every year.

Worth a line.

Exposure, say, US$1 million to US$1.5m, i.e. two or three TLs a year less US$500,000 premium or at most US$1,000,000.

Line 7.5/10% plus treaty if needed.

1995 comment

None.

PROPOSITION 8

SLIP DETAILS

REASSURED: A French company.

PERIOD: 1983 hail season.

TYPE: STOP LOSS.

CLASS: All business written in the reassured's direct hail department.

TERRITORIAL SCOPE: France and all other countries in which the reassured may operate.

TREATY DETAIL: To pay the amount by which aggregate losses exceed 110% of gross net premium income but not exceeding 50% of gross net premium income of F.Frs.8,000,000, whichever is the lesser.
Minimum deductible F.Frs.11,000,000.
Minimum and deposit premium F.Frs.410,000 payable at 50% at 1 May 1983 and 50% at 1 September 1983 adjustable at 4% gross net premium income.

DEDUCTIONS: 10%.

GENERAL CONDITIONS: Ultimate net loss clause.
Net retained lines clause.
Atomic pools exclusion clause.
War and civil war exclusion clause.

WORDING: To be agreed (leading underwriter only).

INFORMATION

Loss Ratios

Exceeding 100%		Last five years	
1950	170%	1978	31%
1955	115%	1979	35%
1968	101%	1980	30%
1971	220%	1981	55%
		1982	82%

Premium income

	1981	F.Frs.11,000,000
	1982	F.Frs.12,000,000
Est.	1983	F.Frs.13,000,000

Company's original commissions: 20%
Company's overheads: 18%
Fruit and vegetables comprised 15% of the account.

ASSESSMENT

Proposition 50% excess of 110% for 4%.
 Historical record over 40 years—two total losses and one loss of 5% in 1955.

Burning Cost $\dfrac{105\%}{40} = 2.6\% \times \dfrac{100}{70} = 3.7\%$

This is mathematically a reasonable proposition but does not really attract me with the last loss in 1971. Next one may be due soon.
 A smallish line of, say 2.5% = F.Frs.200,000 or decline.

1995 comment

The actual loss ratios for years 1983–87 were 100%, 148%, 87%, 40% and 71%.
 So the next big loss "was due soon" and my caution fully justified.
 A small line in 1983 and 1984 increased for 1985 onwards at a 6% rate instead of 4% would have been sensible underwriting.

PROPOSITION 9

SLIP DETAILS

REASSURED:	A first-class Japanese company.
PERIOD:	Continuous contract to attach at 1 April 1984 subject to three months' cancellation notice prior to anniversary date each year. Business in force at termination to run off until natural expiry, unless reinsured elects to withdraw portfolio.
TYPE:	PERSONAL ACCIDENT FIRST SURPLUS TREATY.
CLASS:	In respect of all personal accident business accepted directly by the reassured in Japan including baggage, liability and special expenses endorsements.
TERRITORIAL SCOPE:	Worldwide.
TREATY DETAIL:	To take up to 30 times the retention of the reassured subject to a maximum cession hereunder of Yen 3,000,000,000 any one known accumulation or any one conveyance.
RATE:	Original gross rate.
COMMISSION:	35%.
BROKERAGE:	2.5%.
PROFIT COMMISSION:	20% (deficit carried forward to extinction. Provisional statement after three years, final statement after five years).
CASH LOSS:	Yen 10,000,000.
ACCOUNT:	Half-yearly on underwriting year basis.
WORDING:	To be agreed by leading underwriter.

GENERAL CONDITIONS:	Exclusions:
	    War and civil war.
	    Airline personnel and air-crew accident.
	    Professional sports teams' accident.

Proposition 9

INFORMATION

First Surplus (Yen 000)

	Premium income	Losses	LR
1979	140,000	50,000	36%
1980	200,000	40,000	20%
1981	160,000	64,000	40%
1982	130,000	39,000	30%
1983	150,000	165,000	110%

No major outstanding losses 1984.
 Largest loss—1983 Yen 110m (Korean Air Lines).
 Estimated PI Yen 180,000,000 1984.
 Trip business—85% of which group is 52% part of 85%.

ASSESSMENT

A group aviation travel account with PI of Yen 160m against liability maximum of Yen 3,000m in one crash—i.e. 20 × annual income.

However, record is good and maximum exposure may not often be used.

Profitability is around 30% or Yen 500,000,000 when trips go all right.

The Japanese are usually pretty careful and a line of, say US$120,000 or Yen 30,000,000 part of Yen 3m, i.e. 1%, is about all we should write to give a premium of Yen 1,600,000 or US$6,000.

A bit of a "flyer"—low premium, high limit, but probably low risk, but the premium income is uneconomic so we should decline.

1995 comment

None.

PROPOSITION 10

SLIP DETAILS

REASSURED:	A first-class Japanese company (same as previous 1st surplus).
PERIOD:	Losses occurring during period 12 months at 1 April 1984.
TYPE:	EXCESS OF LOSS.
CLASS:	All personal accident business accepted by reassured in Japan including baggage, liability and special expenses endorsements.
TERRITORIAL SCOPE:	Worldwide.
LIMIT:	Yen 1,200,000,000 any one loss or series of losses arising out of one event in excess of Yen 100,000,000 any one event.
PREMIUM:	Minimum and deposit premium: Yen 8,000,000 payable half-yearly in advance. Adjustable at .30% gross net premium income.
GENERAL CONDITIONS:	War and civil war exclusion clause. Net retained lines clause. Ultimate net loss clause.
WORDING:	As before or to be agreed (leading underwriter only).

INFORMATION

1. Estimated premium income: (1982,83 Yen 3,000,000,000)
   (1983,84 Yen 3,500,000,000)
2. Largest loss from ground: 1983 Yen 40,000,000.

Company has 30-line treaty. Maximum net retention Yen 100,000,000 any one known accumulation. Maximum net retention any one person Yen 25,000,000.

ASSESSMENT

This is a very high limit which seems very unexposed with a maximum known accumulation of Yen 100,000,000—i.e. a total loss would mean 13 times this.

Proposition 10

We have earthquake exposure excess of four people but little exposure on trip travel for this.

The rate on line is under 1% but looked at on basis of, say, four maximum people excess of four maximum people, or one known maximum accumulation excess of one known maximum accumulation, the rate on line is around 10%.

Compare the Yen 10m premium against the Yen 40m a year profit on the first surplus. This looks a better write.

As we have declined the first surplus let us write a 10% hereon with our treaty—i.e. 5% net to us for a net line of US$240,000 and a premium of US$2,400.

1995 comment

None.

PROPOSITION 11

SLIP DETAILS

Note: E$20 = US$1

REASSURED: A South East Asia national reinsurance company.

SCOPE & SOURCE: Each and every policy emanating from all insurance companies in respect of comprehensive and third party liabilities together with allied liability except passenger liability, if any, as original.

PERIOD: Continuous contract commencing 1 January 1985 subject to 90 days' notice of cancellation.

TYPE: QUOTA SHARE RETROCESSION MOTOR.

TREATY LIMITS (100%): Comprehensive E$600,000 each vehicle.
Liabilities: (a) compulsory E$60,000 each person but unlimited each accident;
(b) non-compulsory E$600,000 each accident.
Reassured's retention: 40% of limits.

PREMIUM: To pay and receive as original in every respect.
Reinsurance commission: 5%.
Fee 1%.
Profit commission: 20% with two years' deficit clause (management expenses 5%).

PREMIUM AND LOSS RESERVE: Nil. The reinsured may at discretion call upon the individual reinsurer for LOC issued by sound bank to cover their share of unearned premium and outstanding losses calculated quarterly by the reinsured.

CASH LOSS: Nil.

BORDEREAUX: Nil.

ACCOUNT: Quarterly on underwriting year basis.

OVERRIDER TO REASSURED: 2.5%.

CONDITIONS: All terms, clauses, conditions and warranties and settlements, etc. are as original and to follow the original in every respect.

WORDING: To be agreed by leader.

Proposition 11

HEREON: Acceptance expressed as percentage of 100% of 60% quota share with maximum limits:
Comprehensive: E$360,000 each vehicle
Liabilities: (a) compulsory: E$36,000—e.p.;
(b) non-compulsory: E$360,000—e.a.

INFORMATION

Past underwriting results up to close of 1984 as attached.
Estimated premium income for 100% of 60% QS:

1984 E$1,000 million.
1985 E$1,200 million.

Additional information and comments given by reassured

(1) Reduction of reinsurance commission to 5%.
(2) A general reconstruction of the motor insurance tariff by the local Insurance Association has been submitted for approval to the Insurance Advisory Council of the Ministry of Finance and approval of this is anticipated.
(3) An approximate increase of 15% in all rates is anticipated upon receipt of approval of the tariff changes.
(4) The main points of the tariff reconstruction are:
  (i) motor theft shall be separated from damage to car (DTC) section of the comprehensive motor insurance policy and to be rated separately with a deductible of 30%;
  (ii) premium calculation of DTC shall be based on "replacement cost value"—i.e. new car value irrespective of the age of car;
  (ii) no-claim bonus and surcharges under various circumstances shall be enforced.

The reassured anticipates an EPI for this treaty in 1985 of E$1,200,000,000.

E$000's

Year of account		Premiums received	Accumulated Paid Loss Ratio	
1977	1977	200	26	
	1978	220	77	
	1979	220	83	
	1980		84	
	1981		85	O/S NIL

Proposition 11

E$000's

Year of account		Premiums received	Accumulated Paid Loss Ratio	
1978	1978	320	24	
	1979	340	82	
	1980		87	
	1981		88	
	1982		88	O/S 1%
1979	1980	445	27	
	1981	454	83	
	1982		88	
	1983		89	
	1984		89	O/S 1% Est.
1981	1981	572	24	
	1982	583	79	
	1983		84	
	1984		84	O/S 1.5% Est.
1982	1982	660	27	
	1983	690	88	
	1984	690	93	O/S 3% Est.
1983	1983	700	30	
	1984	730	85	O/S 16% Est.
1984	1984	900	30	O/S 30% Est.

ASSESSMENT

In order to evaluate the trend on this business we need to tabulate the results in the form of a "progression triangle".

Loss Ratios %

Year of Account	Yr. 1	Yr. 2	Yr. 3	Yr. 4	Yr. 5	o/s	Incurred Loss Ratio	My Estimate Final Loss Ratio
			Paid Losses at End of					
1977	26	77	83	84	84	—	84	84
1978	24	82	87	88	88	1	89	89
1979	23	79	82	83	83	1	84	84
1980	27	83	88	89	89	1	90	90
1981	24	79	84	84		1.5	85.5	86
1982	27	88	93			3	96	97
1983	30	85				16	101	103
1984	30					30		105
1985								108

The percentages underlined are our own projected figures.

It is clear that the years 1977 to 1980 show no particular trend with average loss ratios between 84% to 90%.

From 1981 to 1984 there is a steadily worsening trend and if this continues the 1985 loss ratio is inevitably going to be well over 100%, though 108% may be pessimistic.

The figures show that with a 30% settlement at the end of 12 months there will be a balance of premium to invest, but this is only of the order of 50% of the premium for, say, 12 months.

Our costs are:

Minimum commission	5%
Fee	1%
Overrider	2.5%
Total	8.5%

Clearly, to show a profit of 5% to us we need a loss ratio of 86.5% or better. In other words, our estimated 1985 loss ratio of 108% has got to improve by 20%.

We are told that we may get a 15% increase in rates during 1985 but this will only mean at most a 7.5% increase as policies come up during the year. Five per cent or less is more realistic.

Improvement under (4) (i), (ii) and (iii) might have a more dramatic effect but is unquantified.

There seems very little prospect for 1985, so decline and wait for 1986.

1995 comment

None.

PROPOSITION 12A

SLIP DETAILS

REASSURED:	A large UK insurance company.
PERIOD:	Continuous contract from 1 January 1984 subject to 45 days notice of cancellation to 31 December any year. Losses occurring basis.
TYPE:	EXCESS OF LOSS (2ND LAYER).
CLASS:	Motor vehicles. Excluding obligatory treaties other than from nominated locally incorporated subsidiary and/or associated companies. All other exclusions as agreed.
TERRITORIAL SCOPE:	Worldwide, excluding business emanating from sources in the USA and business underwritten by the home department of the reassured.
LIMIT:	To pay up to £250,000 (indexed) ultimate net loss each loss in excess of £250,000 (indexed) ultimate net loss each loss. Index base as at 1 January 1982; at 1 October 1983 index was 118%.
PREMIUM:	Annual minimum and deposit premium £40,000 payable in four equal instalments on 1 January, 1 April, 1 July and 1 October each year, adjustable annually at .50% original gross premium income.
DEDUCTIONS:	10% brokerage.

GENERAL CONDITIONS:	Ultimate net loss clause (amended for underlying £150,000 excess of £100,000).
	Net retained lines clause.
	Excluding:
	    War and civil war, etc.
	    Atomic pools
	    Nuclear incident
	    Excess of loss reinsurances
	72 hours clause:
	    hurricane, typhoon, windstorm, rainstorm, hailstorm and/or tornado

earthquake, seaquake, tidal wave and/or volcanic eruption
riots, civil commotions and malicious damage
168 hours clause—any other catastrophe
GCC claims clause (advice limit £100,000).

WORDING: As before (as far as applicable but taking into consideration any alterations as shown hereon). Any future wording amendments to be submitted to leading underwriter only.

PROPOSITION 12B

SLIP DETAILS

REASSURED: A large UK insurance company.

TYPE: EXCESS OF LOSS (3RD LAYER).

PERIOD: Continuous contract from 1 January 1984 subject to 45 days' notice of cancellation to 31 December any year. Losses occurring basis.

CLASS: Motor vehicles.
Excluding obligatory treaties other than from nominated locally incorporated subsidiary and/or associated companies.

TERRITORIAL SCOPE: Worldwide as underlying.

LIMIT: To pay up to £500,000 (indexed) ultimate net loss each loss in excess of £500,000 (indexed) ultimate net loss each loss.

Index base as at 1 January 1982.

PREMIUM: Annual minimum and deposit premium £20,000 payable in four equal instalments on 1 January, 1 April, 1 July and 1 October each year, adjustable annually at .30% original gross premium income.

DEDUCTIONS: 10% brokerage.

GENERAL CONDITIONS: As underlying.

INFORMATION

Premium income	1979	£4,200,000
	1980	£5,000,000
	1981	£6,000,000
	1982	£7,000,000
	1983	£7,500,000
	Est. 1984	£8,000,000

Income is:	70%	Private cars
	25%	Light commercial
	1%	Coaches

Maximum property damage limit £500,000

	70%	Comprehensive
	30%	Fire, theft and third party

Account	50%	Europe
	10%	Africa
	15%	Canada
	10%	Australia
	15%	Elsewhere

Largest loss to date £300,000 o/s.

ASSESSMENT SECOND LAYER

Whilst we only have one outstanding loss to the layer for 1981 we have losses in 1978, and possibly 1979 and 1980, which could exceed £250,000. Also 1982 and 1983 look as if they will penetrate too.

Our deductible is indexed from 1 January 1983, but is expressed in sterling, and losses are calculated in sterling at 30 June 1983 rates of exchange. There is no currency clause in the event of devaluation of sterling or other movements. This is unusual.

At a premium of £40,000 this should be declined.

ASSESSMENT THIRD LAYER

So far clear of losses though large losses are under-assessed in early years and the outstanding of £300,000 in 1981, £250,000 in 1983 and £200,000 in 1983 could progress to near £500,000. Serious awards may exceed £500,000 per person.

On the other hand the deductible is indexed and may increase to over

£600,000 or so by January 1984. I would assess this as marginal. The rate will produce a premium of just on £25,000.

A line only, because of indexation. I would not write it unindexed. But not too big a line! Five per cent net is enough for a liability of £25,000 or £30,000 against a premium of £1,250.

Note: our liability will rise with indexation.

1995 comment

A wise decision to decline second layer. A terrible decision to write third layer. See proposition 34.

PROPOSITION 13

SLIP DETAILS

REASSURED:	A large German company.
PERIOD:	Continuous contract to attach at 1 January 1985, subject to three months of cancellation to expire at 31 December any one year.
TYPE:	GERMAN MOTOR DAMAGE EXCESS OF LOSS.
CLASS:	To cover motor physical damage business written by the ceding company excluding TP personal accident, passenger liability.
LIMIT:	To pay Dm 1,500,000 excess of Dm 500,000 each and every loss and/or occurrence or series of losses and/or occurrences out of any one event.
REINSTATEMENT PROVISION:	Reinstatement unlimited at pro rata additional premium, but minimum 50% on time.
PREMIUM:	Minimum and deposit premium: Dm 500,000 payable in two instalments on 1 February and 1 August each year. Adjustable at .40%—10% brokerage.
BROKERAGE:	10% nil on reinstatements.
GENERAL CONDITIONS:	Ultimate net loss clause. Net retained lines clause. Nuclear energy risks exclusion clause (reinsurance) (1984) NMA 1975.
WORDING:	As expiring or as co-reinsurers or as agreed.

INFORMATION

Loss record (DM)
    Munich storm 1984 3,500,000 from ground up
                        1982 1,500,000 from ground up
                        1978 2,000,000 from ground up
    75% private cars
    15% commercial
     5% caravans
     5% motorcycles

Largest fleet exposure a.o. garage Dm 2,000,000. Only 10 exceed 1,000,000.

ASSESSMENT

An excess of loss covering physical damage to motor vehicles.

    Past record   1978   1,500,000 hereon
                          1981   1,000,000 hereon
                          1984   1,500,000 hereon

It appears that one can accept a "natural peril" total loss every three years or so, which is to be expected with a deductible of Dm 500,000.

The proposition earns Dm 624,000 or a rate of lines of 42% or 38% after brokerage.

There is little per location exposure.

A real betting proposition. The reinstatement premium is substantial, minimum 20% on line which just about tempts me to "have a go" for 1985 after the bad 1984 year.

A line of 7.5% = US$35,000 a.o. loss for a premium of US$14,000. But the real exposure is, say, three total losses in a year less 100% premium—i.e. one premium at 42% plus three reinstatement premiums at 20% less 10%, i.e. Dm 3,000,000 or US$800,000. So a 7.5% line is a possible US$60,000 exposure. With a 50% cession to our treaty we could accept a gross line of 15%.

1995 comment

None.

PROPOSITION 14

SLIP DETAILS

REASSURED:	A government insurance office.
PERIOD:	Losses occurring during period 12 months at 1 July 1984.
TYPE:	EXCESS OF LOSS CONTRACT (1ST LAYER).
CLASS:	Business written by the reassured in their general third party liability department.
TERRITORIAL SCOPE:	Australia and New Zealand and Mandated Territories. Worldwide for personal liability and also for personnel whilst operating outside Australia but who are normally resident in Australia.
LIMIT:	To pay hereunder up to A$200,000 each and every loss occurrence excess of A$300,000 each and every loss occurrence.
PREMIUM:	Minimum and deposit premium: A$360,000 payable in four equal quarterly instalments. Adjustable at 7.5% on original gross premium income.
DEDUCTIONS:	10% plus Australian tax as applicable.
GENERAL CONDITIONS:	Ultimate net loss clause. Net retained lines clause. Excluding treaty excess of loss reinsurances. War and civil war exclusion clause. Nuclear energy risks exclusion clause (1984). Index clause—base date 1 July 1984.
WORDING:	As expiring or to be agreed (leading reinsurer only). Special acceptances as expiring; any further cases to be agreed (by leading reinsurer).

INFORMATION

Lead by well-known European reinsurance company with 25%.

Proposition 14

Claims record (excess of A$100,000)

			A$	
1974/75	Nil			
1975/76	1 paid at	150,000	TP one person	
1976/77	1 paid at	1,000,000	TP one person	
	1 paid at	400,000		
	1 outstanding	300,000	TP one person	
1977/78	Nil			
1978/79	Nil			
1979/80	Nil			
1980/81	1 paid at	600,000	Driving accident	
1981/82	1 outstanding	500,000	TP accident 2 people	
	1 outstanding	200,000	TP accident 1 person	
1982/83	2 outstanding	120,000	Personal liability	
		500,000	Accident 1 injured	
1983/84	2 outstanding	250,000	TP 1 person	
		1,000,000	Erection collapse	

Above claims indexed on consumer price index as used in the contract would have been as below.

NB In some cases this indexation makes claim exceed the actual policy limit.

		Losses	A$ 200,000 Excess of A$ 300,000	AS$
	1975/76	340,000	40,000	
	1976/77	2,000,000	200,000	
		800,000	200,000	
		600,000	200,000	
	1980/81	800,000	200,000	
	1981/82	600,000	200,000	
		240,000		
	1982/83	132,000		
		560,000	200,000	
	1983/84	270,000		
		1,000,000	200,000	
	Ten Years		1,440,000	
		Average Annual	144,000	
GNPI (estimate)	1983 A$4,000,000			
	1984/85 A$4,600,000			

Based on A$4,000,000 premium income annual BC 3.70%.
Loaded by 100/70 = 5.3%.
But no allowance for IBNR and claims progression?

Previous contract to 1 July 1983 was A$400,000 excess of A$100,000 at rate 2%.

Record over 10 years was premium A$400,000. Losses paid and outstanding A$2,400,000.

For 12 months (1 July 1983) contract was for A$300,000 excess of A$200,000 at 4%.

Original policy limits may go up to A$5,000,000 but majority of policies are for A$500,000 or less.

ASSESSMENT

This is typical of the drastic re-underwriting taking place in 1984 and 1985.

On the basis of the past record, a rate of 7.5% earning A$370,000 should be adequate. It is over 200% of the BC on an indexed basis.

The claims progression is not known but this would appear to be a "pay-back" situation. However, this is a real working layer with full exposure on the majority of policies.

The premium will earn interest as claims appear to take three to five years to settle and no reserves for outstanding losses are called for.

In addition, the deductible and limits are indexed. At this level this will increase both the limit and the deductible. However, the indexation of the deductible is important, in my view.

For a working TP layer this certainly has attractions and a line of 10% means A$20,000 per occurrence. But really the risk is for, say, five total losses in a year for A$1,000,000 hereon = A$100,000 for a premium of A$37,000 less 10%. But note, our line might easily increase to A$30,000 per occurrence; i.e. A$150,000 in all.

So, unless we are brave, perhaps 8% is enough. Not one we should cede to our treaty.

1995 comment

I think I was right but have doubts.

PROPOSITION 15

SLIP DETAILS

REASSURED: A first-class and substantial USA company.

PERIOD: Continuation from 1 July 1984 on continuous contract from 12.01 a.m. Central Standard time, 1 July 1979, covering losses on an occurring or "claims-made" basis as original (except as regards fidelity and forgery with losses discovered basis) subject to 90 days' prior notice of cancellation by either party at any subsequent 1 July.

Coverage shall also apply on an aggregate basis in respect of occupational and other diseases and in respect of original policies with aggregate limits. Such aggregate coverage shall attach at the inception anniversary or renewal date on or after 1 July 1979 and in the event of cancellation, coverage shall continue hereunder until the end of the policy year. Each policy year shall mean each separate original policy period of not exceeding 12 months plus odd time and any other discovery and/or run-off provisions contained in the original policies.

TYPE: CASUALTY EXCESS OF LOSS COVER.

CLASS: Covering the following business including such business under multi-peril package policies:
(1) Workers' compensation, employers' liability and voluntary compensation, all including occupational disease.
(2) All bodily and personal injury liability including professional liability and automobile no-fault and medical payments.
(3) All property damage liability classified as casualty including professional liability.
(4) Fidelity and forgery.
(5) Burglary.

EXCLUSIONS: (1) Aviation liability, unless such coverage forms an incidental part of the original insured operations. However, aircraft products liability shall not be covered when the original policy is issued to a concern principally engaged in the manufacture of aircraft, aircraft engines or aircraft propellers.

(2) Policies covering workers' compensation, general liability and automobile liability business under which the reinsured receives complete reimbursement for all losses and expenses thereunder.
(3) All business of the General and Excess Management Corporation whether assumed directly or indirectly by the reinsured.
(4) Financial guarantee and insolvency.
(5) Liability assumed in the reinsured's reinsurance department.
(6) Excess of loss reinsurance, stop loss reinsurance, quota share and surplus treaty reinsurances assumed from other insurance and reinsurance companies and from Lloyd's syndicates. (This exclusion does not apply to any such reinsurances effected between any of the companies reinsured hereunder nor to liability accepted by the reinsured by way of insurance or pro rata reinsurance in respect of excess of loss insurance nor to acceptances of reinsurances on specific risks).

TERRITORIAL SCOPE: Worldwide as original.

LIMITS: To pay up to US$8,000,000 ultimate net loss each and every loss recurrence excess of US$2,000,000 ultimate net loss including loss adjustment expenses each and every loss occurrence.

Notwithstanding this, cover shall pay up to US$8,000,000 ultimate net loss in the aggregate any one original policy year for each insured and/or hazard excess of:

(1) in respect of products liability (including completed operations), US$4,000,000 ultimate net loss in the aggregate for all loss any one original policy year for each insured;
(2) in respect of all other business subject to aggregate limits, US$2,000,000 ultimate net loss in the aggregate with respect to each hazard or each hazard of each project subject to an aggregate limit;
(3) in respect of occupational or other diseases of one specific kind or class, US$2,000,000 ultimate net loss in the aggregate any one original policy year for each insured;

Proposition 15

(4) in respect of occupational or other diseases of all kinds or classes, US$4,000,000 ultimate net loss in the aggregate any one original policy for each insured.

However, reinsured to retain the first US$3,000,000 of losses each annual period which would otherwise be collectible hereunder.

This aggregate deductible does not apply to directors and officers liability business.

WARRANTY: No claims shall be paid hereunder in respect of workers' compensation, occupational diseases or automobile no-fault claims involving unlimited medical expenses unless two persons have claims of at least US$25,000 each, and two or more persons are involved, or unless such claim is involved in a loss with another line of business covered hereunder. This warranty does not apply to employers' liability which is considered to be a separate line of business from workers' compensation for purposes hereafter.

PREMIUM:
Annual minimum premium: US$6,000,000
Annual deposit premium: US$7,000,000
payable in quarterly instalments
Adjustable at .90% of subject gross net written premium income.

DEDUCTIONS: 15% plus 1% Federal Excise Tax as applicable.

LOSS RESERVES: Agreed allow letters of credit—Citibank Scheme—(to include Evergreen clause) and/or outstanding claims advance if required.

GENERAL CONDITIONS: Ultimate net loss (including 90% extra-contractual obligations loss)—reinsured granted permission to carry underlying excess of loss reinsurances.
Net retained lines clause.
Self-insured obligations clause.
Excess of original policy limits clause.
Extra-contractual obligations clause.
Commutation clause as agreed.
Loss reserves clause.
Insolvency clause.
Errors and omissions clause.
Automatic unlimited reinstatement.
Nuclear incident exclusion clause—liability—reinsurance.
Insolvency funds exclusion clause.

Proposition 15

                        Service of suit clause (as applicable).
                        Extended expiration clause.
                        Claim review if required.
                        Continuity clause.

WORDING: Wording as before as far as applicable or to be agreed.
                        Leading underwriter only.

INFORMATION

Slip is lead in Lloyd's with 7.5% line and supported in Lloyd's.

JULY	1984/85	Subject GNWPI (Est.)	US$800,000,000
	1978/79	GNWPI	US$400,000,000
	1983/84	GNWPI	US$700,000,000

Policy limit profile by number of policies:

Casualty	0 – 2m	8%
	2 – 5m	6%
	5 – 10m	6%
	Over 10m	2%
Professional Indemnity	0 – 2m	70%
	2 – 5m	11%
	5 – 10m	12%
	Over 10m	7%
Burglary Fidelity Forgery	0 – 2m	88%
	2 – 5m	5%
	5 – 10m	5%
	Over 10m	2%

Others under US$2,000,000

Premium income	Casualty	300m
	Professional Indemnity	60m
	Burglary	50m
	Fidelity & Forgery	20m
	WCA	350m
	Others	20m

Loss record

US$

	Excess of 2m		To Layer 8m Excess 2m	After 3m Aggregate
1978/79	5,000,000	paid	3,000,000	
	2,000,000	o/s	Nil	Nil
1979/80	4,000,000	o/s	2,000,000	2,000,000
	5,000,000	paid	3,000,000	
1980/81	10,000,000	o/s	8,000,000	5,000,000
1981/82	6,000,000	o/s	4,500,000	1,500,000
	2,500,000	o/s		
1982/83	3,000,000	o/s	1,500,000	Nil
	2,500,000	o/s		
1983/84	7,000,000	o/s	5,000,000	2,000,000
Totals			**27,000,000**	**10,500,000**
Average per Annum			**4,500,000**	**1,750,000**

ASSESSMENT

First excess

This is very heavy stuff with about 15% of the premiums exposed by number and much greater volume by proportion of the premium income.

The tail of this business will be considerable, particularly on general third party side, workmen's compensation and professional indemnity.

The effect of the aggregate deductible must be very carefully considered as it raises an important rating principle that is worthwhile analysing in some detail.

> Premium income   1978/79   US$400 million
> 1983/84   US$700 million

Using interpolation for 1979/80 to 1982/83 we can get out the Burning Cost for US$8 million excess of US$2 million and for US$8 million excess of US$2 million plus a US$3 million aggregate deductible.

The US$3 million deductible should be looked at as a percentage of premium income in past years and I have therefore included a column with an aggregate deductible of US$3 million expressed as a percentage of the 1984/85 premium income of US$800 million—i.e. the US$3 million aggregate becomes worth .375% of each past year's income and *not* a flat US$3 million as shown in the slip information viz:

1978/79	US$1,500,000	1981/82	US$2,100,000
1979/80	US$1,650,000	1982/83	US$2,400,000
1980/81	US$1,800,000	1983/84	US$2,700,000

Therefore we can calculate three Burning Costs as follows:

US$

Year	GNWPI in Millions	Losses 8m Excess of 2m	Less 3m Aggregate	Less .375% Aggregate or Deductible
1978/79	400	3,000,000	Nil	1,500,000
1979/80	440	2,000,000 3,000,000	2,000,000	3,350,000
1980/81	480	8,000,000	5,000,000	6,200,000
1981/82	560	4,500,000	1,500,000	2,400,000
1982/83	640	1,500,000	Nil	Nil
1983/84	720	5,000,000	2,000,000	2,300,000
Total	3,240	27,000,000	10,500,000	14,750,000
Burning Cost		.87%	.32%	.46%
Loading 150%		1.3%	.48%	.69%
Deduct value of 3m deductible at .375%		.925%	.48%	.69%

Now, if the loading of 150% is correct, and we will comment on that below, then which of these three results is the most sensible? In my view, there is only one answer—the Column 3 loaded rate of .925%. One should not give up one's loading on that portion of losses which falls within the aggregate deductible. Any rating based on Column 4 will be quite inadequate and Column 5, though better, is still illogical.

Now we have stated that this is a very long-tail account and the IBNR factor will be large. Therefore a loading of 150%, which might be reasonable on a property short-tail account, does not take into account the inevitable claims progression and the deductible is unindexed.

Without having the past claims progression we will have to estimate but our loading should be of the order of not less than 200% on the Burning Cost of 1.3% for a minimum rate of 2.6% less .375% or 2.25% against a contract rate of .80%. Clearly this contract is badly underrated and we decline even though a premium of US$6,400,000 gives a good potential of earning interest.

I question whether any rate based on past experience makes any sense at all on a proposition of this nature.

The premium income from policies in range of US$2 million–US$5 million is:

Casualty	6% × US$5m	=	18	million
Professional Indemnity	11% × US$60m	=	6.6	million
Fidelity, etc.	5% × US$20m	=	<u>1</u>	million
			25.6	million

We will need 10% of that—i.e. US$2,500,000 for policies US$5m to US$10m

   18   million
  7.2 million
  <u>1</u>   million
26.2 million

We will need 20% of that—i.e. US$5,000,000 for policies over US$10 million

  6   million
4.2 million
<u> .4</u> million
10.6 million

We will need 33.33% of that—i.e. US$3,300,000 for a total of US$11 million plus the WCA aggregate exposure.

So our total premium should be in the region of US$15 million or a rate of 2%, and even this may prove to be inadequate given the very long-tail inherent in this type of business and the probable inadequacy of the original rates.

1995 comment

I am sure I was right to have nothing to do with this, with unlimited reinstatements, claims are still rolling now.

PROPOSITION 16

SLIP DETAILS

REASSURED: A substantial and conservative USA mutual company.

PERIOD: Continuation covering losses occurring from 12.01 a.m. 1 July 1984 on continuous contract from 12.01 a.m. 1 July 1980 subject to 90 days' cancellation clause at any 1 July. Losses occurring basis, except as regards aggregate reinsurance provisions and except with respect to any coverages written on a losses discovered or claims-made basis.

TYPE: THIRD CASUALTY EXCESS OF LOSS COVER.

CLASS: All business classified by the reassured as casualty business including personal, professional commercial umbrella business and excess business and fidelity business (when written separately or as part of homeowners multi-peril business). Burglary, miscellaneous surety and yacht protection and indemnity but excluding automobile physical damage including collision, contract surety, boiler and machinery, accident and health and life.

EXCLUSIONS:
(1) Workers' compensation and employers' liability in respect of underground coal mining operations. Notwithstanding this exclusion, minor coal mining operations, which are incidental to risks falling within the scope of this contract, are covered hereunder.
(2) Financial guarantee and insolvency.
(3) Any risks written by the company's aviation department or written by the company as a member of an aviation insurance group or risks of which the flying hazard is a major part.
(4) Product liability on risks engaged in the manufacture of aircraft or of completed aircraft engines.
(5) Any operations which include:
fireworks manufacturing
fuse manufacturing
  Manufacturing of any explosive substance intended for use as an explosive. (*Note:* an explosive substance is defined as any substance manufactured for the express purpose of exploding as differentiated from other com-

modities used industrially and which are only fortuitously explosive, such as gasoline, celluloid, fuel gases and dyestuffs.)

Manufacturing of any products (other than fireworks and fuse) in which any explosive substance (as detailed above) is an ingredient.

Loading of any such explosives substance (as defined above) into containers for use as explosive objects, propellant charges or detonating devices and the incidental storage thereof.

(6) Excess of loss reinsurance.
(7) War risks, where applicable.
(8) Business written in the company's reinsurance department.
(9) Nuclear incident exclusion clauses, where applicable.

And, with respect to commercial umbrella business and excess business only:

(10) Pharmaceutical risks where contraceptives are involved.
(11) Chemical risks which involve herbicide manufacturing.
(12) Rail roads.
(13) Gas utilities.
(14) Oil and gas exploration, refining and drilling.

And, with respect to fidelity/burglary business only:

(15) Financial institutions.
(16) Fiduciary liability under Employers Retirement Income Security Act of 1974.

With respect to exclusions 1, 3, 4, 5, 10, 11, 12, 13 and 14, they do not apply with respect to risks which are regularly engaged in other operations, a minor part of which involves the excluded operations, nor where an insured, after attachment date of a policy, acquires premises or commences operations or develops products which are excluded by these exclusions until 30 days (subject to statutory requirements and policy terms) after the date when authorised underwriting personnel of the company are advised of such activity.

If risks falling within the scope of the above exclusions are assigned to the company under an Assigned Risk Plan, the coverage afforded by this contract shall apply to such risks but not in respect of limits greater than those prescribed by said Assigned Risk Plan.

If the company, without the knowledge and contrary to the instructions of its managerial or supervisory staff is bound on a risk falling within one of the above exclusions, such risk is covered for a further period of thirty (30) days (subject to statutory requirements and policy terms) after the receipt of such knowledge by such personnel of the company.

LIMIT:

To pay US$3,500,000 ultimate net loss each and every loss excess of US$2,500,000 ultimate net loss each and every loss, except as regards aggregate reinsurance features. With respect to policies written on a "Losses Discovered" or "Claims-Made" basis, this reinsurance to follow original as to date of loss.

In addition to occurrence protection hereunder, the reinsurance limit and retention also to apply on aggregate loss basis each original policy year where original policies provide aggregate limits and in respect of occupational or other disease. This aggregate reinsurance shall apply to original policies written, renewed or having anniversary after 1 July 1984.

Policy year shall mean each separate original policy period of not exceeding 12 months as from inception, anniversary or renewal date. In the event of termination, liability hereunder shall cease at the next anniversary date of such policies following the date of termination of this reinsurance.

TERRITORIAL SCOPE:

Worldwide.

PREMIUM:

Annual minimum and deposit premium US$900,000 payable in four quarterly instalments.
Adjustable at rate .70% of gross net earned premium income.

DEDUCTIONS:

Less 15% and 1% Federal Excise Tax as applicable.

LOSS RESERVE:

Letters of credit Citibank scheme—if required.

GENERAL CONDITIONS:

Ultimate net loss clause (including expenses and including 80% extra contractual obligations)—amended.
Excess of original policy limits clause.
Self-insured obligations clause.
Extra-contractual obligations clause.
Insolvency funds exclusion clause.

WORDING: Wording as before or to be agreed by leading underwriter only.

INFORMATION

Premium

		US$000
Estimated Premium Income		150,000
Split	WCA	70,000
	Commercial Liability including Umbrella	40,000
	Fidelity	10,000
	Personal Liability	5,000
	Burglary	20,000
	Miscellaneous	5,000
Maximum	Commercial Liability including Excess	5,000
	Fidelity	5,000
	Burglary	2,500
	Personal Liability and Miscellaneous	1,000

Under 5% Liability and Fidelity policies are for limits over US$2,500,000.

Loss progression

US$000

Losses exceeding US$2m over past ten years.

1975	Nil paid or outstanding	
1976	First advised 1978	US$1,500,000 outstanding
	First advised 1979	US$1,500,000 outstanding
	First advised 1980	US$2,500,000 outstanding
	First advised 1983	US$2,000,000 settled
1977	Nil paid or outstanding	
1978	First advised 1980	US$3,000,000
	Settled 1982	US$3,000,000
1979	Nil	
1980	Nil	
1981	Nil	
1982	First advised 1983	US$2,000,000
	First advised 1984	US$2,600,000 o/s
1983	One outstanding at US$3,000,000	
1984	Nil	

Losses hereon
1976	Nil paid
1978	US$500,000 paid
1982	US$100,000 outstanding
1983	US$500,000 outstanding

ASSESSMENT

Premium hereon approximately US$1,050,000.

Their estimates look good on settlement. A much less heavy account than Proposition 15 and policies exposed are small.

The professional indemnity income is not there and a premium of just over a million dollars looks reasonable.

I think a modest line is justified but we shall have to watch the exposure by policy limit each renewal and also the progression of past results. Net line, say, 1% for an exposure of US$35,000 and a premium of US$10,000.

No treaty cession in view of long-tail.

1995 comment

On reflection I would have been better off declining this.

PROPOSITION 17

SLIP DETAILS

REASSURED: A substantial Eastern Bloc reinsurer.

PERIOD: Continuous cover always open for full amount for losses occurring between 1 January 1985 and 31 December 1985 both days inclusive Central European Time.

INTEREST: FIRST MARINE AND AVIATION GENERAL EXCESS OF LOSS CONTRACT excluding:
(a) hull insurance on aircraft unless previously advised and a special premium, to be agreed, paid;
(b) all reinsurances;
(c) building risks on vessels building for Democratic Socialist Republics but including trial trips thereon.

LIMITS: To pay up to US$10,000,000 any one ultimate net loss or series of losses arising from one event in excess of US$1,000,000 any one ultimate net loss or series of losses arising from one event.
Subsidiary limits any one event in incidental non-marine branches:
(a) Import and export machinery and erection risks US$4,000,000.
(b) Other incidental non-marine business US$2,000,000.
(c) Aviation, excluding hulls but including liabilities (whatsoever nature) US$10,000,000.
Losses falling under more than one category—limit hereunder US$10,000,000 excess of US$1,000,000.

REINSTATEMENT: One at 50%. One at 100%. Thereafter held covered.

CONDITIONS: Original conditions.
All risks and conditions as original but:
(a) warranted original war risk insurances on hull interests to be subject to automatic termination of cover clause as London Market;
(b) London Market trading warranties for hull war risks dated 1 October 1983;
(c) war inclusion clause 1976;
(d) 72 hours clause for windstorm, tidal wave and earthquake.

WORDING:		Contract wording as expiring or as agreed.	
PREMIUM:		US$4,000,000 payable in four equal and separate instalments at 1 January 1985, 1 July 1985, 1 October 1985 and 1 April 1986.	
BROKERAGE:		10.5%.	

Wording includes:
(a) Ultimate net loss and net retained lines clauses amended to provide for protection of any quota share reinsurers.
(b) Settlement of losses in US dollars at official rates.
(c) Exclusion of atomic risks and liability arising from nuclear accidents but including transits as wording.

INFORMATION

1. Fleet list with insured values furnished at inception and changes and additions will be reported monthly.
   Advices will be given of building and repairing risks if insured value exceeds US$5,000,000.
2. Aircraft passenger liability will be covered at the Hague Protocol/ Warsaw Convention limits, where applicable, but in any event not exceeding US$20,000 per person.

US$000

	Premium	Claims Paid	Claims Outstanding
1975	1,700	—	—
1976	2,000	1,272	—
		941	
1977	2,100	602	—
1978	2,600	192	—
1979	2,600	686	—
		—	—
		—	—
1980	3,000	5,120 TL	—
		2,108 TL	—
		—	
1981	3,000	2,780 TL	—
		—	
1982	2,500	510	—
		—	
		—	300
		—	—

		Premium	Claims Paid	Claims Outstanding
	1983	3,000	233	—
		—	—	—
	1984	3,000	—	3,295
		—	—	—
			—	3,800
		—	—	—
TOTAL		25,500	14,444	7,395

US$000

1985 Estimated premium income—US$12,000,000.

ASSESSMENT

A substantial marine and aviation excess of loss treaty for a major Eastern Bloc insurer, covering all marine and aviation risks.

Pros

Reinsurance exclusion, non-accumulative. Reasonable overall premium/ overall loss ratio. 1–3 if two reinstatements used. Pay-back rate available to a new reinsurer as well after 1984 total losses. Information level on hull exposures. Losses occurring cover basis.

Cons

A flat premium, which is dangerous for such an obvious risk excess as a dramatic increase in original premium could alter the risk enormously. 100% underwriting. It is apparent from the losses that the reassured are a policy insurer rather than a line writer.

Potential problem with "Held Covered" provision on reinstatement.

I reckon this could have a "PML" of two total losses a year—i.e. US$20,000,000 against a premium of US$6,000,000. So we are writing a contract loss of US$14,000,000 or, if we increased the assessment to three total losses—i.e. US$30,000,000 less US$10,000,000, a loss of US$20,000,000.

A line of .75% net plus, say, an equal cession to our treaty or a gross 1.5% for a maximum estimated PML line of US$150,000 net against a premium of US$30,000.

1995 comment

None.

PROPOSITION 18

SLIP DETAILS

50 Southland $ = US$1

REASSURED:	A third world national company.
TYPE:	SECOND SURPLUS.
INTEREST:	Hull and machinery and/or hull interest all as original and as accepted by reassured as hull risk. Warranted Southland FOM.
TREATY CONDITIONS:	All terms, clauses and conditions as original. Orders in excess of retention of reassured plus capacity of first Surplus. Excluding war risks.
LIMIT:	S$300,000,000 any one hull and pro rata on interest (not exceeding 25%) surplus to capacity of First Surplus and retention.
PERIOD:	1st January to 31st December 1985.
WORDING:	As agreed leader only. ILU to sign treaty wording on behalf of all member companies subject prior agreement leading company.
PREMIUM RESERVE:	10%. Interest 4.25%. Released at 12 months.
LOSS RESERVE:	Nil.
ACCOUNTS:	Quarterly. Deposit premium S$1,000,000 payable within three months of inception of treaty.
CASH LOSSES:	S$1,000,000.
PROFIT COMMISSION:	10%. 4% management expenses. Losses carried forward to extinction.
RATE:	Original gross rate (to be agreed with two leading underwriters from Lloyd's and companies prior to attachment for new and/or added vessels and current joint hull understanding to be applied for renewals).

COMMISSION INCLUDING BROKERAGE:	25%.
TAXES:	As original, if any. Agreed authorise LPSO and/or ILU and/or PSAC to allocate signing date and number and take down premiums, etc. and claims, etc., prior to wording documents being signed. Deposit premium S$1,000,000 payable within three months of inception of treaty.

STATISTICS AT 30 SEPTEMBER 1984

Figures for 100%

Currency: Southland $

Underwriting Year	Net Premium	Paid Claims	O/S at 31.12.83
1978/79	8,426	67	—
1980	3,727	—	528
1981	1,812	—	782
1982	7,415	—	152
1983	9,236	—	—
1984	5,912	—	—
1985 est.	11,000	—	—

ASSESSMENT

Second surplus hull treaty for a third-world national insurer.

Pros

Excellent results, probably only a few of the national fleet's newest and best vessels at this level.
  Average discounts and low profit commission.
  At face value good cash flow.
  Rating control by leaders.

Cons

Lack of balance. Income/limit ratio—30:1. No information on attachments.

This is not really a treaty and we should treat it as a facultative reinsurance.

Therefore, we should not accept unless we either have bordereaux or a schedule of risks and only accept if we are satisfied as to the rating and quality of the original business.

If we were to accept I would like to keep our line to US$150,000 (our maximum PML line). On the top exposure this means 2.5% of Southland $300,000,000. In US$ a top line of US$150,000 for a premium of US$5,000.

We could use our treaty for 2.5% making a gross written line of 5%.

1995 comment

None.

PROPOSITION 19

SLIP DETAILS

REASSURED:	A Japanese company.
PERIOD:	Continuous cover always open for full amount applying to the reassured's underwriting account for 1984 and subsequent underwriting years. Subject to three months' notice of cancellation expiring 31 March, of any one year.
TYPE:	SPECIAL HULL FIRST SURPLUS TREATY.
INTEREST:	Hull and/or machinery and/or interest in respect of vessels owned by or bareboat chartered to overseas companies wholly or partly owned by Japanese interests, etc. Maximum Yen 3,000,000,000.
TREATY CONDITIONS:	Original conditions, but free of capture and seizure.
WORDING:	Contract wording as expiring or as agreed by leading reinsurers.
ACCOUNT:	Quarterly.
CASH LOSS:	Yen 100,000,000.
PROFIT COMMISSION:	10% losses carried forward three years.
RATE:	Original gross rates.
COMMISSION:	15% or ONR on captive accounts where original commission exceeds 15% as far as applicable.
BROKERAGE:	2.5% on gross or on ONR where applicable.
INFORMATION:	Estimated net premium 1983 Yen 600m 1984 Yen 600m The reassured have signed "respect the lead" underwriting. Provisional declarations in respect of cession of Yen 1,500,000,000 and over hereto.

Figures for 2% written line

Yen 000

As at 31.10.83 (1979/82)
31.03.83 (1972/78)

Year	Net Premium	Claims Paid and O/S
1972	3,878	1,437
1973	4,732	3,857
1974	12,725	11,092
1975	17,974	12,659
1976	12,247	15,842
1977	8,745	10,938
1978	6,798	7,789
1979	6,262	6,537
1980	6,347	13,287
1981	7,658	14,862
1982	13,231	7,762

ASSESSMENT

Pros

Comparative balance. Income/limit ratio of 5:1. Not much else. Modest commissions, good cash flow.

Cons

Described as surplus but operated as facultative obligatory. Japanese ownership qualification not restrictive enough. Falls into less attractive category of treaties of this type.

Poor results, evidence of the substantial underwriting of this business since the mid-1970s; the treaty is too balanced for the results to be explainable by unlucky frequency of total losses.

Would decline.

1995 comment

Quite right.

PROPOSITION 20

SLIP DETAILS

B$20 = US$1

REASSURED:	State insurance corporation.
PERIOD:	Losses occurring during 12 months at 1 January 1985.
TYPE:	EXCESS OF LOSS (2ND LAYER).
INTEREST:	All cargo business written in the marine department of the reassured.
TERRITORIAL SCOPE:	Worldwide.
LIMIT:	B$12,000,000 Ultimate net loss each and every loss and/or series of losses arising out of one event. In excess of: B$3,000,000 Ultimate net loss each and every loss and/or series of losses arising out of one event.
WARRANTY:	National insurance corporation retain B$1,000,000 any one policy, but B$4,000,000 any one bottom for bulk cargo only.
REINSTATEMENT:	Two reinstatements at 100% of final earned premium.
PREMIUM:	B$360,000 in full.
BROKERAGE:	10% (nil on reinstatement).
GENERAL:	Subject to original terms, clauses and conditions and to follow settlements and/or agreements of reassured in all respects. Ultimate net loss clause. War inclusion clause 1976.
EXCLUSIONS:	(1) Hull or vessel or aircraft for time of voyage unless carried as cargo. (2) Freight disbursements, time charter hire, premium, outfits, advance stores, if insured for time. (3) Ocean tows of any description of interest written as such.

Proposition 20

(4) Excess of loss insurance other than those on reporting basis.
(5) Contingency risks.
(6) Rejection and confiscation risks.
(7) Package deals (but when cargo is rated separately the cargo section to be included) and manufacturers output risks.
(8) All other interests (cargo excepted) insured for time.
(9) Obligatory treaties.

WORDING: Wording as before as far as applicable, or to be agreed by leading underwriter only.

INFORMATION

Estimated gross net premium income 1985—B$50,000,000. Largest past loss 1979—B$3,500,000 (Port Fire).

ASSESSMENT

Catastrophe cargo business excess of loss for an African insurer (on retention under treaties). Likely to consist mainly of imports of manufactured goods and machinery and construction materials: possibly of some exports of ores or minerals or foodstuffs such as coffee, etc.

Pros

Fair quality third-world catastrophe risk.

Exposure level likely to be low with the warranted policy limits (but single vessel exposure is just possible).

Non-aggregated business, easy to identify any potential clashing lines. Comprehensive exclusion but probably designed for their pro rata treaty.

Cons

Low vessel lines typical of these sorts of risks. Possibility of substantial warehouse accumulations (fire risk).

Verdict

A line of 15% ceding 7.5% to our treaty for a net line of US$45,000 and a net premium of US$1,350.

1995 comment

None.

CHAPTER 7

UTOPIAN REINSURANCE 1983–1989: UNDERWRITING EXAMPLES 1988–1989

The Utopian started quietly in 1983. Our 1983 and 1984 years were both underwriting losses covered by our investment income; an inauspicious start. However, our income increased to US$12,000,000 in 1985. 1985, 1986 and 1987 were exceptionally profitable years. Our 1985 year made an underwriting profit of 25% and 1986 33% on an income of US$18,000,000. 1988 was also profitable. We had established substantial loss reserves by the end of 1988 and our capital and surplus had grown to US$25,000,000.

This was increased to US$40,000,000 by raising an additional US$15,000,000 of paid-in capital. We had an investment fund of capital, reserves and premiums of over US$50,000,000 yielding us US$5,000,000 a year.

We had increased our line limits from US$300,000 to US$1,000,000 by 1988 and for 1989 to US$1,200,000. This represented 3% of our estimated 1989 income of US$40,000,000 and also 3% of our capital.

The years 1985 and 1986 saw dramatic changes in liability reinsurance. Due to the continued deterioration of asbestos losses and the emergence of pollution claims, it was no longer possible to purchase global reinsurance programmes (those which responded to both property and liability claims). In addition the greater use of claims-made basis and the re-underwriting of liability business made it more attractive. As a company since 1983 we had written a predominantly physical damage account but during the late 1980s we did write some volume of liability or casualty business. When we set our liability line guides in 1989 we not only took into account our overall premium income and surplus of $40,000,000 but also the liability income itself, which represented about 15% of our account or $6,000,000. Therefore, we set our maximum line per programme at 10% of that or $600,000 (50% of our normal limits).

We had to purchase a separate casualty outwards reinsurance programme and as this was very expensive from 1986 onwards, we bought very limited coverage.

Apart from our entry into liability and casualty business, our underwriting gradually broadened both by class and by territory.

ANALYSIS CODES

It had become apparent after a few years that we needed to improve our coding structure. The advent of personal computers and the need to analyse the portfolio in more detail meant that we introduced various refinements.

(1) It was necessary to give each individual contract a separate reference number. This would allow for easy separation of any contracts in dispute or showing particularly adverse experience.

(2) It was necessary to code the business to closely match that required by the regulatory authorities and reinsurers.

(3) Following the problems of asbestosis and pollution and the increased development of claims-made policies, we decided to introduce "reserving codes" that helped to define the expected tail of the portfolio written.

(4) We decided to introduce more territorial codes to account for the development of our portfolio in Australasia, the Far East and other territories.

These developments showed the importance of having flexible computer and coding systems enabling us to make these changes with the minimum of inconvenience.

During this time we also improved our computer system to produce triangulated statistics. These were produced separately by each underwriting year and enabled us to compare any code or group of codes between underwriting years. These triangulations showed the development of not only premiums but more importantly paid losses and incurred losses.

PROPOSITION 21A

SLIP DETAILS

REASSURED:	The Fantastic Insurance Company Ltd. and/or its nominated locally incorporated subsidiary and/or associated companies.
PERIOD:	12 months from 1 January 1989. Losses occurring during basis.
TYPE:	EXCESS OF LOSS.
CLASS:	The home foreign account of the reassured.
TERRITORY:	Worldwide, excluding USA unless incidental.
LIMIT:	To pay up to £500,000 ultimate net loss each and every risk in excess of £500,000 ultimate net loss each and every risk.
REINSTATEMENT:	One at 50% A.P., two at 100% A.P. for time, pro-rata for amount.
PREMIUM:	Minimum and deposit premium £196,000 payable in four equal instalments on 1 January, 1 April, 1 July and 1 October 1989. Adjustable at 2.45% of the gross net premium income.
BROKERAGE:	10% (nil on reinstatement).

GENERAL CONDITIONS:	Ultimate net loss clause.
	Net retained lines clause.
	Excluding:
	    War and civil war, etc.
	    Hail on growing crops.
	    Bonds, forgery and fidelity.
	    Nuclear energy risks exclusion clause (reinsurance) 1984. NMA 1975 (Japanese amendment).
	Currency fluctuation clause (or t.b.a. L/U only).
	Run-off clause at terms to be agreed.
	Special acceptances to be agreed by leading underwriter only and to include automatically on renewal any special acceptances from the previous year.

WORDING: To be agreed by leading underwriter only.

PROPOSITION 21B

SLIP DETAILS

REASSURED: The Fantastic Insurance Company Ltd. and/or its nominated locally incorporated subsidiary and/or associated companies.

PERIOD: 12 months from 1 January 1989. Losses occurring during basis.

TYPE: EXCESS OF LOSS.

CLASS: The home foreign account of the reassured.

TERRITORY: Worldwide, excluding United Kingdom and USA unless incidental.

LIMIT: To pay up to £3,000,000 ultimate net loss each and every risk in excess of £1,000,000 ultimate net loss each and every risk.

REINSTATEMENT: Two at 100% A.P. for time, pro rata for amount.

PREMIUM: Minimum and deposit premium £255,000 payable in four equal instalments on 1 January, 1 April, 1 July and 1 October 1989. Adjustable at 3.25% of the gross net premium income.

BROKERAGE: 10% (nil on reinstatement).

GENERAL CONDITIONS: Ultimate net loss clause.
Net retained lines clause.
Excluding:
    War and civil war, etc.
    Hail on growing crops.
    Bonds, forgery and fidelity.
    Nuclear energy risks exclusion clause (reinsurance) 1984 NMA 1975 (Japanese amendment).
Currency fluctuation clause (or t.b.a. L/U only).
Run-off clause at terms to be agreed.
Special acceptances to be agreed by leading underwriter only and to include automatically on renewal any special acceptances from the previous year.

WORDING: To be agreed by leading underwriter only.

PROPOSITION 21

INFORMATION

Premium income

				£000
1980	3,200	1985	7,300	
1981	4,800	1986	7,100	
1982	5,700	1987	7,400	
1983	5,900	1988	8,700 assumed	
1984	6,200	1989	8,900 estimated.	

Limits

£2,250,000 for class 1 risks.
Minimum 25% MFL.

Classes

Property and Pecuniary classes, excluding Liability.

Projected 1989 income for home foreign

	£000
Europe	1,670
Middle East	1,210
Far East	770
Africa	900
Caribbean	870
Worldwide	980
South America	1,120
Australasia	810
Other	570
	8,900

Risk profile by sum insured

All policies in force on 21 September 1988.

£000	Number of risks	Premiums in £m
0– 500	970	3.20
500–1,000	530	1.22
1,000–2,000	250	0.78
2,000–3,000	177	1.82
3,000–4,000	135	1.83
4,000–5,000	47	0.62
Over 5,000	136	1.52
Totals	2,245	10.99

Home foreign account

£

Claims exceeding £250,000

			Excess of 500,000
1980	—	—	—
1981	—	—	—
1982	Hotel Royal	335,000	—
1983	Ariel	296,000	—
1984	—	—	—
1985	Lefton	574,000	74,000
	Hill Anderson	265,000	—
	Shortsense	404,000	—
1986	Smith and Davidson	183,000	—
1987	Fortune Hotels	885,000	385,000
	Saudi Arabia Factory	487,000	—
	Plastic Foam Furniture	444,000	—
1988	Tetra-pak	631,000	131,600
	P T Sallen	348,000	—
	ICI South Africa	321,000	—

QUESTIONS

Q. Is the £2,250,000 class I limit a risk or MFL limit?

A. MFL see risk profile.

Q. Does this include pecuniary loss?

Proposition 21   123

A. Yes.

Q. How long has this been in force and what was maximum MFL limit in 1985 and 1987? Is any change anticipated?

A. Introduced in 1988.
No change for 1989.
1985 £1,500,000 maximum EML.
1987 £1,750,000 maximum EML.

ASSESSMENT

We are not asked to quote or lead this proposition so our assessment must be fairly quick.

As a leader this would require in-depth analysis of exposures to each layer and of past losses. Here we will do two quick assessments and if these support the quoted terms and we trust the leader we will take a line, if not we will decline.

PART 1

Past loss record

This must be indexed in some way.
  (a) Line limits have gone up 50% in four years.
  (b) P.I. has gone up 45% in five years.
  (c) Our cost of building index has risen 60% in five years (my assumption).

Therefore I shall index up losses as follows, and use years 1984 to 1988 inclusive.

£

	Losses			1st Layer	2nd Layer
1984	Nil				
1985	574,000 + 50%	=	861,000	361,000	—
	265,000 + 50%	=	398,000	—	—
	404,000 + 50%	=	606,000	106,000	—
1986	183,000 + 37.5%	=	—	—	—
1987	885,000 + 25%	=	1,060,000	500,000	60,000
	487,000 + 25%	=	609,000	109,000	—
1988	631,000 + 12.5%	=	710,000	210,000	—
	348,000 + 12.5%			—	—
	321,000 + 12.5%			—	—
			Totals	1,286,000	60,000

This produces an average annual cost to 1st layer of (500,000 × £500,000) of £257,000. Load this by 100/75 = £343,000.

So our premium for 1st layer ought to be around £350,000 or rather less giving credit for reinstatement APs: say £320,000/£330,000 or rate 3.6%.

PART 2

As percentage of exposed premium income

£000

Risk Breakdown for Layer	1st Layer—Exposure	Premium to Layer
500–1,000	Average Exposure 750 1st layer 250 × 500 33.33% × 66.66% Worth 10% of exposed premium income of 1,200	120
1,000–2,000	Average Exposure 1,500 1st layer 500 × 500 33.33% × 33.33% Worth 17.5% of 800	140
2,000–3,000	Average Exposure 2,500 1st layer 20% × 20% Worth 20% of 820	160
3,000–4,000	Average Exposure 3,500 1st layer 14% × 14% Worth 20% of 830	160
4,000–5,000	Average Exposure 4,500 1st layer 11% × 11% Worth 20% of 620	120
over 5,000	Average Exposure 6,000 say 1st layer 8% × 8% Worth 15% of 1,500	<u>225</u>
	Total	925
	Less 30% commission Less, say, 25% for EML being 25% less than sum insured	650 **490**

Conclusion on 1st layer

Both assessments are 50% (or more) higher than offered terms.
Therefore decline. No argument.

1995 comment

A correct decision.

2nd layer

Virtually no losses.

£000

Risk Breakdown for Layer	2nd Layer—Exposure	Premium to Layer
1,000–2,000	Average 1,500 2nd layer 500 × 1,000 33.33% × 66.66% Worth 8% of 800	64
2,000–3,000	Average 2,500 2nd layer 1,500 × 1,000 60% × 40% Worth 20% of 800	160
3,000–4,000	Average 3,500 2nd layer 2,500 × 1,000 70% × 30% Worth 25% of 800	200
4,000–5,000	Average 4,500 2nd layer 2,500 × 1,000 57.5% × 12.5% Worth 25% of 600	150
Over 5,000	Average 6,000 2nd layer 40% × 17% Worth 25% of 1,500	375
	Total	949

Total gross exposed premiums, say, £950,000
Less 30% commission £670,000
Less EML discount, which on this layer could be 40% £400,000
or rate of 4% on PI.
Slip terms are 2.95% to produce £260,000/270,000.

I regard our £360,000 price as heavily discounted and reinstatements will be small and would not discount further so *decline as well.*

PROPOSITION 22

SLIP DETAILS

CEDING COMPANY:	Hereford Insurance Company.
CLASS OF RISK:	Property damage and pecuniary loss.
FORM OF TREATY:	Surplus.
TERRITORY:	Worldwide (excluding USA, Canada, Germany, unless incidental and Home Foreign).
TOTAL NUMBER OF LINES:	12.
RETENTION OF CEDING COMPANY:	Top £400,000 (EML) Property Damage or £400,000 (EML) Pecuniary Loss but limited to £600,000 (EML) if written jointly—scaled down by class and construction.
ESTIMATED PREMIUM INCOME:	1989—£14,200,000.
TREATY LIMIT:	£8,000,000 (EML) scaled down by class and construction.
COMMISSION:	35%.
PROFIT COMMISSION:	20% of net profit exceeding 5% of premium income. Five year Deficit Clause.
RESERVES:	Nil.
PORTFOLIOS:	Incoming At 1.1.89 35% premiums 90% outstanding claims. Outgoing At 31.12.89 35% premiums 90% outstanding claims.
PERIOD:	Continuous at 1.1.89 subject to three months' annual notice of cancellation to 31 December.
ACCOUNTS:	Quarterly.
CLAIMS REPORTING LIMIT:	£150,000 for 100% of treaty.
CASH LOSS LIMIT:	£250,000 for 100% of treaty.
WORDING:	As 1988.

INFORMATION

Property Damage and Pecuniary Loss business is confined to risks of physical loss or damage to property and consequential loss arising therefrom in respect of our commercial and industrial portfolios.

The treaty excludes:

1. Motor.
2. Lineslips unless specially agreed by leading reinsurer.
3. Liability.
4. Binding authorities.
5. Captive accounts.
6. Space risks.
7. Fidelity guarantee.
8. Marine and aviation business including goods in transit business unless underwritten in the property account.
9. Contractors all risks policies issued in the name of the Channel Tunnel Consortium.

A pollution exclusion is being incorporated in all new UK fire and consequential loss policies and into renewals as from August 1988.

ASSESSMENT

We are offered a line on a take it or leave it basis. *Our assessment must be quick.*

Top EML limit £5,000,000. Gross income £14,000,000. Fairly well balanced on EML basis but not on a risk basis. Terms 35%, no brokerage. On high side, 30% in my view is enough, or 32% with brokerage.

PC and deficit—reasonable
no reserves—good
portfolio transfer—reasonable
cash loss—on low side.

Results (See p. 129)

Disastrous up until 1985. From then on good. Average profit around 15% on £14,000,000 is £2,000,000 odd which is 40% of maximum EML limit—not impressive.

There is no risk limit, only an EML limit and no maximum EML stated. Our view must be determined by our feeling as to 1989 and future prospects, i.e. what is happening to original rates in the market.

The general pressure is downwards and in spite of 1988 experience I am against this one by feel. Either decline, or if you don't want to put off the broker or the company, a small line only, say 0.25% or 0.5%. I don't like terms, i.e. 35%

commission or an unlimited risk exposure and 1989 or 1990 may well see a downturn in their results.

0.5%	= £70,000	premium income
Max EML exposure	= £25,000	
Max annual loss, say 30% of PI	= £21,000	
Possible annual profit	= £10,500	

A 0.25% line is more than enough for me.

Conclusion

Decline or write not more than 0.25%.

1995 comment

None.

HEREFORD INSURANCE COMPANY

FIRST SURPLUS PROPERTY DAMAGE AND PECUNIARY LOSS TREATY (ACTUAL)

8 LINES FOR YEARS 1982/1987
12 LINES FOR YEAR 1988

	1977/81 (inclusive)	1982	1983	1984	1985	1986	1987	½ year 1988
PREMIUMS	22,285,123	5,298,942	6,598,186	8,476,623	9,720,191	12,093,496	14,185,414	7,320,492
INCURRED CLAIMS O/S ESTIMATED AT 90%	12,984,042	4,024,061	5,138,196	6,970,414	4,863,729	5,891,126	6,892,824	3,723,209
COMMISSION	7,924,867	2,101,072	2,612,870	3,412,896	3,414,260	3,724,410	4,242,801	2,220,428
PORTFOLIO	872,941	26,127	361,410	705,342	434,967	689,999	589,027	—
BALANCE (BEFORE P.C.)	503,273	(852,318)	(1,514,290)	(2,612,029)	1,007,235	1,787,961	2,460,762	1,376,855
	22,285,123	5,298,942	6,598,186	8,476,623	9,720,191	12,093,496	14,185,414	7,320,492
PROFIT/(LOSS) RATIO	2.26%	(12.92%)	(22.96%)	(30.81%)	10.36%	14.78%	17.35%	18.81%

PROPOSITION 23A

SLIP DETAILS

TYPE:	Self-funded medical and hospitalisation expense plan specific excess insurance.
FROM:	J(A) plus AIF 719 plus application form dated 10 January, 1988 AIF 719(E).
ASSURED:	St Swithin Health Centre, California.
PERIOD:	From 1 January 1988 to 1 January 1989 both days at 12.01 a.m. Local Standard Time.
INTEREST:	Claims incurred under the assured's plan during the policy period and paid during the policy period or the 90 days immediately after the end of the policy period.
SUM INSURED:	$650,000 per person in excess of $50,000 per person.
SITUATION:	As per policy wording.
CONDITIONS:	Administration to be carried out by ABC Life Company.

PREMIUM:	$80,000 (Minimum & Deposit) payable $20,000 each quarter, in advance and adjustable at expiry at:
	     $3.75 per employee with single coverage
	     $7.50 per employee with employee plus one dependant coverage
	     $11.25 per employee with family coverage.

BROKERAGE:	20%.
INFORMATION:	Number of lives at inception—Single: 1,000 plus E + 1: 260 plus family: 330 Total of 1,590. Lead by experienced Lloyd's leader with 20% slip well supported.

PROPOSITION 23B

SLIP DETAILS

TYPE:	Self-funded medical and hospitalisation expense plan aggregate excess insurance.
FROM:	J(A) plus AIF 718 plus application form dated 20 May 1988 plus endorsements AIF 718(A), AIF 718(G)—weekly indemnity.
ASSURED:	Acme Engineering Co., Georgia, USA.
PERIOD:	From 1 January 1988 to 1 January 1989 both days at 12.01 a.m. Local Standard Time.
INTEREST:	Claims paid under the assured's plan during the policy period.
SUM INSURED:	$1,000,000 in the aggregate excess of: 　Either 130% of the Expected Claims Cost 　Or $150,000 　whichever the greater.
SITUATION:	As per policy wording.
CONDITIONS:	Administration to be carried out by XYZ Life Company. Expected claims cost calculated at: 　$57.65 per month per employee with single coverage and $172.95 per month per employee with family coverage. 　Maximum any one person under the plan $15,000.
PREMIUM:	$3,500 (Minimum and Deposit) payable at inception and adjustable at expiry at 3% of the expected claims cost.
BROKERAGE:	20%.
INFORMATION:	Number on lives at inception 　Single:　　50 　Family:　　51 　Total of:　101 Lead with 20% by the experienced Lloyd's leader and well supported.

PROPOSITION 23

ASSESSMENT

Technically these are insurances, but in practice they are reinsurances of a fund.

These examples illustrate a dilemma met by many underwriters such as ourselves.

We have no great technical knowledge of this type of business. However, it is short-tail business, it will widen our account and it will not be additional to most of our business and it is not accumulative unless there is a plague (AIDS?).

I would discuss this business with the leading underwriter whom I know and, provided I trust him, will follow him on the rating and him alone.

The line I can write may be determined by the brokers, but we should contact all brokers on this class to achieve as wide a base as possible "following the lead".

The main thing here is to ensure:

(1) That the rates are adequate and based on a proper actuarial base.
(2) That the scheme is properly serviced and administered.
Note the condition in each contract.

As to lines, the aggregate contract with a limit of $1,000,000 is very little exposed. All the risk is in the first $100,000, so I would write 15% to 20%, which will have to be an exception to our minimum premium of $1,000, which is justified, as our costs will be low.

The excess per person with a limit of $650,000 per person is much more exposed and could easily have a TL or even two in a year. The premium reflects this; a line of 5% to 7.5% looks enough.

1995 comment

None.

PROPOSITION 24

SLIP DETAILS

REASSURED:	Bald Eagle Insurance Co.
PERIOD:	12 months losses occurring from 1 April 1989.
TYPE:	CATASTROPHE EXCESS COVER (1ST LAYER).
CLASS:	Covering all business classified by the reassured as property including, but not limited to automobile physical damage, boiler and machinery, glass, ocean and inland marine, and to include workers' compensation/employers' liability losses arising out of fire, lightning, explosion, collapse, freeze, windstorm, hail, flood, earthquake, volcanic eruption, riots, strikes, civil commotion or malicious damage.
TERRITORIAL SCOPE:	Anywhere in the United States and Canada.
LIMIT:	To pay up to $12,500,000 each and every loss occurrence excess of $40,000,000 ultimate net loss each and every loss occurrence.
WARRANTY:	In respect of workers' compensation/employers' liability—maximum any one person $4,000,000.
REINSTATEMENT:	One reinstatement at pro rata additional premium for all perils.
PREMIUM:	Minimum premium $1,911,000. Deposit premium $2,249,320 payable quarterly adjustable at 0.2122% gross net earned premium income for 1989 calendar year.
DEDUCTIONS:	Brokerage 15%.
EXCLUSIONS:	1. Loss to growing and standing timber. 2. Ordinary and group life insurance. 3. Financial guarantee and insolvency. 4. War risks as per wording. 5. Insolvency funds exclusion. 6. Nuclear exclusion clause.

	7. All surety bonds.
8. As respects property—business excluded by the pools, association and syndicates exclusion clause (amended).
9. Occupational disease.
10. Seepage and pollution exclusion clause.
GENERAL CONDITIONS:	Warranted 5% co-reinsurance kept by reassured.
Net retained lines clause.
Ultimate net loss clause (amended for underlying reinsurance), including loss expenses and 80% extra contractual obligation loss.
Agreed value commutation clause—workers' compensation/employers' liability only.
Service of suit clause (USA).
Insolvency clause.
Arbitration clause.
Errors and omissions clause.
Extra contractual obligations clause.
Self-insured obligations clause (amended).
Currency clause (amended).
OTHER LAYERS OFFERED:	Rate
Layer 2 15,000,000 ×   52,500,000 .1726% gnepi
Layer 3 15,000,000 ×   67,500,000 .1330% gnepi
Layer 4 17,500,000 ×   82,500,000 .1114% gnepi
Layer 5 30,000,000 × 100,000,000 .1415% gnepi

All with 5% co-reinsurance.
Layers 3, 4 & 5 reinstatement is one at 100% additional premium. |

INFORMATION

Synopsis of cover

Layer	Limit	Deductible	Rate	$ Premium	R.O.L.
1	12.5	40.0	0.2122	2,249,320	18.0
2	15.0	52.5	0.1726	1,829,500	12.2
3	15.0	67.5	0.1330	1,409,800	9.4
4	17.5	82.5	0.1114	1,180,840	6.75
5	30.0	100.0	0.1415	1,500,000	5.0

1989/90 Premium income base

	$000
Homeowners	260
Inland Marine	40
Auto PD Ex Collision	120
Commercial Multiple (property)	160
Commercial Fire	80
Workers' Compensation	400
Total	1,060

1987 California earthquake aggregates

			$ million
Area	Zone	Net Liability	Net PML
San Francisco	A	760	670
Los Angeles/Orange County	B	1160	125
Santa Barbara	C	250	16
San Diego	D	100	20
South-East	E	300	22
Central	F	71	11
North-Central	G	117	20
North	H	7	2

Catastrophe losses

		$000
Greater than $5,000,000		
Cat No.	Date of Occurrence	Net Incurred as of 31/12/88
74	3/4 April 1974	5,900
27 Frederick	12/13 September 1979	10,000
22	7/10 May 1981	5,400
15 Alicia	17/20 August 1983	25,500
24 US Freeze	17/30 December 1983	19,000
32	27/29 March 1984	5,800
56	19/22 January 1985	6,000
81 Elena	30 August, 3 September 1985	10,100
82 Gloria	26/27 September 1985	15,200

State breakdown for major states

	Homeowners %	C.M.P. %
Alabama	0.9	1.0
Arizona	0.5	1.4
California	6.0	12.0
Colorado	1.0	1.2
Connecticut	5.0	3.5
Florida	5.0	5.6
Georgia	1.3	3.4
Illinois	2.0	2.7
Indiana	0.9	1.4
Louisiana	1.5	2.2
Maryland	1.4	1.6
Massachusetts	4.6	3.7
Michigan	2.5	2.5
Missouri	1.0	1.7
New Jersey	4.5	3.4
New York	19.0	17.5
North Carolina	4.0	3.5
Ohio	2.2	2.0
Oklahoma	0.6	1.1
Pennsylvania	5.6	5.5
Rhode Island	1.4	1.0
South Carolina	1.0	1.0
Tennessee	2.0	2.1
Texas	14.5	4.4
Virginia	2.5	3.0
Wisconsin	0.7	1.7
Others	8.4	9.9

Additional information (inserted by us)

Reassured's maximum limit any one risk or plant site is US$12,500,000 and their maximum PML $5,000,000.

ASSESSMENT[3]

A major East Coast US company writing heavily in New York, New Jersey and Pennsylvania as well as New England plus Florida and the South East, Texas and California. Relatively light in the Middle West and Louisiana.

This is a physical damage only catastrophe excess and one notes that WCA & EL are only included for specified perils with a warranty per person of

---

3. 1989 assessment made before Hurricane Hugo.

$4,000,000 and an exclusion of occupational disease and seepage and pollution.

The slip is for the first layer of a programme consisting of five layers of cover. All five layers have been lead and rated by respectable leads and we are offered all five layers.

Our underwriting decisions are therefore fairly simple. Do we think the programme is well underwritten and adequately rated? Which layers should we underwrite and how much should we take?

First, then, read the slip and its clauses. It covers property business with WCA and EL limited as above and is therefore a short-tail proposition. There is one reinstatement only. The exclusions look sensible.

General conditions

Note the qualifications to the ultimate net loss clause with inclusion of extra contractual obligations at 80%. We should ask what underlying reinsurance exists and if possible have that stipulated to ensure that the $40,000,000 deductible is basically a net retention.

The agreed value commutation clause for WCA and EL will shorten our tail and is sensible. The other conditions look reasonable.

Loss occurrence is not defined and we should ask for this definition. It is the standard definition including hours clauses.

There is no limit per risk or by PML in the general conditions or in the information. On enquiry this is a maximum PML of $5,000,000 with a maximum per risk or location of $12,500,000, which we can insert in the information and do so.

Appreciation

First the exposure on a single plant looks very nominal. It could only occur with a major plant wipeout costing $15,000,000 with associated automobile, boiler, IM, WCA & EL totalling over $25,000,000.

The exposure to a conflagration or riot again does not look too serious, it is, however, there. For example, a city centre riot or a major port explosion could involve the lower layers.

The winter freeze exposure is significant and the 1983 December freeze cost then just on $20,000,000, which could approach $40,000,000 on 1990 values. The two major exposures are the Californian earthquake and the windstorm, hail and flood exposure. It is on these we should concentrate.

Earthquake

It is clear from their earthquake aggregate that a major earthquake in San Francisco or in Southern California, i.e. at either end of the San Andreas fault is likely to produce a total loss on all layers. It is possible that the top layer might not be a total loss, but this appears unlikely bearing in mind the extra losses from inland marine, which will include bridges & dams, automobile, ocean marine and possibly WCA & EL.

An earthquake caused by a slip in a minor fault, for example around Los Angeles or San Diego area, is in my view unlikely to cause a $50,000,000 loss and very unlikely to reach $100,000,000.

Even with modern study of the San Andreas fault the next major quake may happen in 1990 or it may not happen for decades or centuries. One thing is certain, it will happen one day. San Francisco happened in 1908 and there was a major quake at the southern end 50 years before that. We argued in 1958 that a quake in Southern California was due. That was 30 years ago.

If you believe it is imminent then this whole proposition is not for you. I reckon the odds are still around 50 to 1, i.e. it should happen within 50 years or so. So an earthquake rate on line of around 2.5% to 3% is not unreasonable. Probably 2% to 2.5% on the top layer and 3% to 3.5% on the bottom layer.

Windstorm flood and hail

Tornado

The spring tornado hail and flash flood risk occurs mainly in the Mid-West from Texas northward. My assessment here is that the risk of loss excess of $40,000,000 is not great and excess of $100,000,000 is remote.

Hurricane

The summer and autumn hurricane risk is, however, very serious. A major hurricane like 1938 or 1944 in New England must produce a loss of over $40,000,000. An East Coast hurricane hitting Pennsylvania and New York the same. A Florida hurricane will exceed $40,000,000 but might not reach $100,000,000. A Texas hurricane with a homeowners income of $40,000,000 in that state could produce a loss around $100,000,000. The only area where a loss might not reach $40,000,000 is Louisiana.

We have the loss experience since 1974:

Frederick	1979	10,000,000
Alicia	1983	26,000,000
Elena	1985	10,000,000
Gloria	1985	15,000,000

Now all these are historically minor hurricanes compared to the Florida hurricane in the 1920s or the 1938, 1944, 1954 and Betsy 1965 hurricanes. Even so, Alicia today could cost them over $40,000,000. My feeling is that it is odds on that a hurricane costing them $50 million to $70 million will happen in the next five to seven years or so and one costing $100,000,000 in the next 15–20 years or so. I think the exposure to loss in excess of $100,000,000 exists on the East Coast and possibly Texas or, of course, New England. I would not have thought that Florida alone with a homeowners income of $13,000,000 and CMP of $10,000,000 should exceed $100,000,000.

Therefore setting out percentage rate on line by perils exposed.

Rate on line

%

Perils	Layer 1	Layer 2	Layer 3	Layer 4	Layer 5
Risk Exposure	—	—	—	—	—
Conflagration					
Explosion					
Riot	1.25	1	0.5	—	—
Winter Freeze	3	1.75	1	0.5	0.25
Earthquake	3.25	3	3	2.5	2.25
Tornado					
Hail					
Flood	1.5	0.75	0.25	—	—
Hurricane	15	9	7	5	3.5
Totals	**24**	**15.5**	**11.75**	**8**	**6**

These are my theoretical rates on line for each layer.

Mine	24%	15.5%	12%	8%	6%
Actual Offer is	18%	12.2%	9.4%	6.75%	5%

The comparison makes the whole programme thinly rated but, bearing in mind a competitive market and practice rather than theory, the offered rates are surprisingly close to mine!

Now look at the top layer: it is a "long" layer of $30 million compared to layer 4 of $17,500,000. If one divided this 30 million into two layers

of   15m × 100m
and   15m × 115m

the premium of $1,500,000 might be allocated as follows:

15m × 100m   Premium $900,000
15m × 115m   Premium $600,000

The $15m × $100m rate on line is 6%, which compares favourably with the 6.75% rate on line on layer 4.

My own view is to miss layers 1 and 2, and perhaps to write layer 3 for a modest line and layer 5 with a proper line. Neither layer justifies writing a maximum commitment and I definitely feel that layers 1 and 2 are too cheap. Using our treaty for a 50% cession on each we should write:

		0.50% of 15m × 67.5m layer 3 = $75,000
plus		1% of 30m × 100m layer 5 = $300,000
line	gross	$375,000
	net	$187,500

1995 comment

Not a wise decision, see Proposition 30.

Authors' note

This Proposition 24 is an excess of loss contract to a direct writing company. Proposition 25 is an excess of loss to a company writing excess of loss reinsurance but not LMX. Proposition 26 is an excess of loss to a company writing excess of loss reinsurance on excess of loss reinsurance including LMX.

The reader should note the effect of gearing, illustrated below:

US$ million

Proposition	Premium Income			Alicia % to PI
24	1,000	Alicia	25	2.5
25	20	Alicia	3.6	18
26	30	Alicia	24	80

PROPOSITION 25

SLIP DETAILS

REASSURED: A London based operation.

PERIOD: Losses occurring during 12 months at 1 January 1989.

TYPE: GENERAL CATASTROPHE EXCESS OF LOSS REINSURANCE.

CLASS: Whole Account.
Excluding the reassured's interest whether direct or by way of reinsurance in loss arising from claim or claims against an insured by another party or parties. Notwithstanding the foregoing, this reinsurance shall not exclude:
  (A) Workers' compensation and/or employers' liability losses arising from the following perils: Fire, lightning, explosion, structural collapse, windstorm, hail, flood, seismic activity, volcanic eruption, collision, riots, strikes, civil commotion, malicious damage.
  (B) Occurrences involving aircraft or parts or equipment relating thereto.
  (C) Any physical damage and/or consequential loss coverage contingent thereon effected by an insured on behalf of another party.

TERRITORIAL SCOPE: Losses wheresoever occurring.

LIMIT:
(For 100%)
Only to pay the excess of an ultimate net loss of £3,500,000 or US or Can$7,000,000 each and every loss and/or catastrophe and/or calamity and/or occurrence and/or series thereof arising out of one event.
To pay up to a further £2,750,000 or US or Can$5,500,000 each and every loss and/or catastrophe and/or calamity and/or occurrence and/or series thereof arising out of one event.

CO-REINSURANCE
WARRANTY: 5% to be retained nett and unreinsured.

WARRANTIES: Not applicable.

REINSTATEMENT: One full reinstatement at pro rata (as to indemnity only) or 75% additional premium.

PREMIUM: (For 100%)	10.7% of the reassured's so-called United States and Canadian Dollar, and Non-Dollar Physical Damage Catastrophe Premium Income accounted for during the period hereon. To be adjusted as soon as practicable after expiry. Minimum and deposit premium: £425,000 plus US$750,000 payable in four equal quarterly instalments on account in advance at 1 January 1989, 1 April 1989, 1 July 1989 and 1 October 1989.
DEDUCTIONS:	10% brokerage—but 5% on reinstatement.
LOSS RESERVE:	Not applicable.
GENERAL CONDITIONS:	Ultimate net loss clause. Benefit of underlying clause. Currency settlements clause "A" (amended as expiring). Run-off clause as expiring. Errors and omissions clause (as expiring). Inspection of records clause (as expiring). Extra contractual obligations inclusion clause (NMX 100). Excluding excess loss reinsurance of Lloyd's underwriters and fringe companies (other than facultatives. Excluding loss or damage directly caused by war and/or civil war but only as regards those classes of business to which the War and Civil War Exclusion Agreement and War and Civil War Risk Exclusion Agreement apply. Nuclear energy risks exclusion clause (reinsurance) (1984), NMA 1975 (Japanese amendment) and nuclear incident exclusion clauses—reinsurance USA and Canada. Canadian dollar claims shall be payable by Lloyd's underwriters in US dollars, the intermediary buying Canadian dollars and collecting the United States dollar equivalent (however, this condition shall not apply if reinsuring underwriters have received Canadian dollar premium in respect of this reinsurance).
WORDING:	As may be agreed by leading underwriter only.

INFORMATION

Loss experience

	Overall Income	Cat. Losses	
1983	£34,500,000	Alicia	$3,600,000
		Cat. 24	$4,000,000
1984	£35,625,000		
1985	£38,625,000	Elena	$1,600,000
		Gloria	$1,500,000
1986	£55,125,000		
1987	£57,000,000	Cat. 87A	£0,900,000
		Cat. 87J	£9,100,000
		Edmonton tornado	Can$1,500,000
1988	£49,500,000		
1989	£42,000,000		

Breakdown of income

US Cat.	$6,400,000
Canadian Cat.	$1,500,000
Non $ Cat.	£4,500,000
US Risk	$7,500,000
Non $ Risk	£2,250,000
US Pro Rata	$6,000,000
Non $ Pro Rata	£1,087,500

Line sizes per programme

US Cat.	$1,500,000	
Non $ Cat.	£2,000,000	
US Risk	$3,500,000	TSI/$1,000,000 PML
Non $ Risk	£2,250,000	TSI/£0,750,000 PML

(Any one assured)
Fac. US	$1,000,000
Fac. Non US	£0,750,000

Aggregates

Nationwide	$64,000,000
Mid-West	$20,000,000
East Coast	$18,000,000
West Coast	$5,000,000
Gulf	$7,000,000
S.E. and Florida	$4,100,000
Hawaii	$3,800,000
Australia	£28,000,000
Caribbean	£25,000,000
Japan	£20,000,000

ASSESSMENT[4]

This account covers both direct and reinsurance business and includes a large excess of loss account both in USA and worldwide, but it does not cover LMX or any reinsurances of Lloyd's or fringe London companies.

The rate is based on catastrophe premium alone, while the policy covers the whole account.

Both the coverage and premium are expressed in US$, Can$ and £ Sterling, which will include all other currencies. I would view this as two covers. US and Canadian and Rest of the World and while some of the US$ income may come from outside the USA we can, for assessment purposes, ignore that.

Taking the USA and Canadian first, the coverage is $5,500,000 × $7,000,000 on a premium income of US$6,400,000 plus Can$1,500,000 giving a total of $7,900,000. The rate is 10.7% of this or $840,000.

There have been no losses since 1983 but Alicia and Cat. 24 both cost around $4,000,000 and, with inflation, might well cost around $7,000,000 each today.

With aggregate exposure for nationwide writing companies of $64,000,000 a 15% loss plus losses on other classes will produce a Total Loss to this policy. The risk exposures excess of $7,000,000 looks remote, so we could put the odds down like this:

A medium or above sized hurricane hitting the US coast anywhere from Texas to New England would cause a Total Loss	15%
Earthquake	2.5%
Mid West Tornado	5%
Others, Conflagration, Riot, Flood	2.5%
Total	20%

4. 1989 assessment made before Hurricane Hugo.

Add for profit and brokerage and we need a premium of $1,300,000.

The premium offered is, therefore, far too low.

Now the Rest of the World, the cover is £2,750,000 × £3,500,000. The rate is 10.7% of premium income of £4,500,000, i.e. £480,000 or about 17%.

Cat. 87J the S.E. England hurricane cost £9,100,000, which was a huge loss and shows the big exposures in the UK. While this was a very exceptional storm, there remains a heavy UK and European exposure to storm, flood and winter freeze plus conflagration or explosion.

My rate for all these is	8%
plus Australia with exposures of, say, £28,000,000	2.5%
plus Japan typhoon, flood and earthquake with exposures of £29,000,000	2.5%
plus Caribbean hurricane and earthquake with exposures of £32,000,000	6%
plus Rest of the World, say,	2%
Total	21%

for a premium of £650,000 allowing for brokerage and profit.

Both sections are too cheap, so decline.

1995 comment

A wise decision.

PROPOSITION 26

SLIP DETAILS

REASSURED: A London based operation.

PERIOD: 12 months at 1 January 1989, losses occurring during basis.

TYPE: EXCESS OF LOSS REINSURANCE.

CLASS: General excess in respect of non-marine account.
Excluding:
(a) Life business, other than accidental death and dismemberment.
(b) Financial guarantee and insolvency.
(c) The reassured's interest whether direct or by way of reinsurance in loss arising from claim or claims against an insured by another party or parties.
Notwithstanding the foregoing this reinsurance shall not exclude:
(i) Worker's compensation and/or employers' liability losses arising from the following perils: Fire, lightning, explosion, structural collapse, windstorm, hail, flood, seismic activity, volcanic eruption, collision, riots, strikes, civil commotion, malicious damage.
(ii) Occurrences involving aircraft or parts or equipment relating thereto.
(iii) Any physical damage and/or consequential loss coverage contingent thereon effected by an insured on behalf of another party.

TERRITORIAL SCOPE: All losses wheresoever occurring.

LIMIT: £3,334,000 or US$ or Can$5,000,000 each and every loss in excess of an ultimate nett loss of £16,666,000 or US or Can$25,000,000.

CO-REINSURANCE WARRANTY: 10% co-reinsurance to be retained net and unreinsured.

REINSTATEMENT: One full reinstatement at pro rata (as to indemnity only) of 100% additional premium.

PREMIUM:
(for 100%) Adjustable at 2.5% of the reassured's so-called Fire Excess of Loss Account Net Premium Income 1989, accounted for during the period of this reassurance. To be adjusted as soon as practicable after expiry.

Proposition 26

	Minimum and deposit premium: £195,000 plus US$292,500 payable at 1 January 1990.
DEDUCTIONS:	Brokerage 10% (reinstatement 5%).
GENERAL CONDITIONS:	Ultimate net loss clause (amended to allow reassured to have benefit of underlying recoveries on other excess of loss contracts so far as applicable).
	Currency conversion clause.
	Definition of each and every loss.
	Errors and omissions clause (as expiring).
	Inspection of records clause (as expiring).
	Nuclear energy risks exclusion clause (reinsurance) (1984), NMA 1975 (Japanese amendment).
	Nuclear incident exclusion clauses—reinsurance—USA and Canada.
	Non-marine London Market war exclusion clause (1978).
	London Market E.C.O. inclusion clause (NMX 100).
	Run-off clause at terms to be agreed.
	Canadian dollar claims shall be payable by Lloyd's underwriters in US dollars, the broker buying Canadian dollars and collecting the US dollar equivalent.
WORDING:	To be agreed by leading underwriter only.

INFORMATION

Overall income

1986	£14,400,000
1987	£16,300,000
1988	£15,300,000
1989	£17,300,000

Cat. losses

1983	Alicia	$23,500,000
	Cat. 24	$19,100,000
1985	Gloria	$1,900,000
1987	87J	£13,000,000
1988	Gilbert	£1,500,000

Breakdown of income (1989)

Generals inc. LMX	£4,125,000
Generals exc. LMX	£1,237,500
Back-ups	£0,577,500
US Cat.	$1,608,750
R/I Assd.	$1,155,000
US Risk	$1,608,750
Non $ Risk	£3,547,500
US Pro Rata	$1,237,500
Non $ Pro Rata	£2,970,000

Aggregates

USA	Nationwide	$68,000,000
	North East	$9,200,000
	North Central	$7,100,000
	South East	$4,400,000
	West Coast	$4,000,000
Australia		£30,000,000
Caribbean		£7,200,000
Japan		£10,000,000

ASSESSMENT

This proposition, unlike the previous one, includes LMX business with a very significant volume. It is, therefore, business where a large loss will take a long time to develop and will be additional to all our own book.

On principle, we should decline this one as we shall merely be taking in our own washing. But for fun we will assess it.

The coverage is in dollars $5,000,000 × US$25,000,000.

Both Alicia and Cat. 24 today would produce a Total Loss and any major US disaster will do the same, so our premium cannot realistically be less than $1,250,000 for a rate on line of 25%.

In £ coverage is £3,334,000 excess of £16,666,000.

Catastrophe 87J cost £13,000,000.

The specific Australian, Caribbean and Japan exposures are fairly light, but the LMX exposures in those areas could be huge.

I would regard the Non US as much less exposed than the US, but it must merit a rate of, say, 6% on line.

The 1989 income is £17,300,000 which at a rate of 2.5% produces a premium of £450,000.

Our premium is 25% of $5,000,000 or $1,250,000 plus 6% of £3,334,000 or £200,000 for a total premium of around £1,000,000.

I am obviously overcharging, but £450,000 seems ridiculously low, so decline.

1995 comment

A wise decision. This is a typical "spinal" LMX contract which caused so many problems in 1989 and 1990.

PROPOSITION 27

SLIP DETAILS

REASSURED: A Lloyd's marine syndicate.

PERIOD: Twelve months at 1 April, 1989. Losses occurring during basis Local Standard Time at the place where the loss occurs.

TYPE: EXCESS LOSS REINSURANCE.

INTEREST: To pay all losses which may be sustained by the reassured howsoever and wheresoever arising but only in respect of the reassured's Excess Loss Reinsurance Account.

LIMITS: Policy for £1,100,000 or United States or Canadian $1,650,000 each loss etc. as defined.
Excess of £2,200,000 or United States or Canadian $3,300,000 each loss etc. as defined.

REINSTATEMENTS: Two reinstatements each at 100% additional premium, in currency of the loss.

CONDITIONS/WORDING: Full wording as EXEL 1.1.89 with additional clauses, deletions, endorsements, special conditions and warranties (at no additional premium) as follows:
War included.
Extra-contractual obligations included.
Non-marine liability exclusion clause 1.10.87 (amended) in respect of original risks attaching on or after 1 March 1987 (included).
Aggregate voyage extension clause (cargo) included.
Aggregate clause (as attached).
Premium adjustment clause (as attached).
Recoveries from any underlying layers to this contract covering the same subject matter as defined in section C of the schedule shall not be deducted in calculating the net loss for the purpose of this contract.
Seepage and pollution exclusion clauses amended under 8.2.2.4 to "Aviation Policies subject to clauses no less restrictive than Aviation Seepage and Pollution Exclusion Clause 11 (1988 amendment)".
It is warranted that all excess of loss treaty reinsurances covering non-marine accounts accepted by the reassured shall for the purpose of this

Proposition 27

	reinsurance be deemed to contain the non-marine casualty exclusion clause. Settlements clause 1987 (XL on XL) in respect of aviation business.
PREMIUM:	Minimum and deposit £70,000 split £21,000 plus US$ 72,000 plus Can$1,500 payable in four equal quarterly instalments in advance but Canadian dollars payable in full at inception. Adjustable at 3.75% of the reassured's 1989 net premium income for all years of account—10% brokerage.
ADDITIONAL LAYER OFFERED:	£1,000,000 excess of £3,300,000. Min and dep Premium £55,000. Rate 3%–10%.

INFORMATION

Schedule C underlying layers

£

500,000 × 150,000	5 Reinstatements
600,000 × 600,000	3 Reinstatements
1,000,000 × 1,200,000	2 Reinstatements

Losses (not limit or warranty)

£

	Net premium income	Aggregate gross paid and o/s losses
1985	£1,000,000	£100,000
1986	£1,200,000	140,000
1987	£1,700,000	570,000 (estimated)
1988	£1,600,000	2,300,000 (estimated)
1989	£1,800,000 (estimated)	

The above incomes include the reassured's participation in quota share treaties protecting an original excess loss account for a total estimated premium income in 1989 of £580,000. Such quota share treaties have the benefit of specific XL reinsurance protections.

Excess of loss portfolio split approximately 57% LMX–43% Foreign.

Past experience

£

Over £100,000

Date of loss	Loss	Losses paid and O/S F.G.U.
17.8.83	Hurricane Alicia	101,000
20.9.84	West Venture	126,256
18.8.86	Hailstorm damage	112,857
6.3.87	Herald of Free Enterprise	127,184
15.10.87	UK Storm	104,057
7.12.87	Rig 55	115,331
18.1.88	Ensenada	164,401
24.4.88	Enchova	190,453
6.7.88	Piper Alpha	1,773,892

Dollars converted at $2.20 = £1.00 1983–1986
$1.50 = £1.00 1987/88

Previous years terms based on PI of £1,600,000.

	Min & Dep	Rate
£1,100,000 × £2,200,000	£25,000	1.60%
£1,000,000 × £3,300,000	£18,000	1.00%

ASSESSMENT 1989

This is an excess of loss on an excess of loss account. Therefore, it is highly volatile and will be additional to our other marine and rig exposures.

However, since Piper Alpha, marine excess loss rates have doubled or trebled and this should be a favourable time to make a small book of this business and either run it net with a strict limit on our aggregates exposures, say, of £500,000 over all such contracts, or purchase excess protection ourselves excess of that figure and increase our aggregate limit.

Turning to the two layers offered.

Layer £1,100,000 × £2,200,000

The Min and Dep premium should apply. This is £70,000 and produces a rate on line of 6.5%.

The layer is £430,000 over the Piper Alpha loss of £1,770,000 but at this stage estimates for Piper Alpha may increase and I would assume that it may well reach our deductible of £2,200,000 eventually.

Proposition 27

It is a factor that on LMX accounts large losses circulate and recirculate for up to four or five years, increasing all the time. We have no information as to the aggregate total of liability. However, assuming an average rate of 10% this would be £18,000,000 at 5% £36,000,000, so a 20% loss or a 10% loss would produce a TL here on the next major disaster.

It does not attract me.

Layer £1,000,000 × £3,300,000

Min and Dep premium of £55,000 will apply and produce a rate of 5.5% on line. The deductible here is nearly twice the Piper Alpha loss and as the 1989 premium income is not much more than the 1988 income the reassured must be reducing his commitments.

However, if one is to write LMX excess R/I such as this, it is essential to know the whole reinsurance programme and its cost. In this case it is:

£500,000 × £150,000	Cost £200,000	5 reinstatements
£600,000 × £600,000	Cost £100,000	
£1,000,000 × £1,200,000	Cost £100,000	
£1,100,000 × £2,200,000	Cost £70,000	
£1,000,000 × £3,300,000	Cost £55,000	
	Total Cost £525,000	

The cost of losses in the first £150,000 were:

1988	£600,000
1987	£570,000
1986	£140,000
1985	£100,000

If one takes an average figure of, say, £350,000 the reassured's position in a good year without a big loss is as follows:

PI £1,800,000	
Cost of first £150,000	£300,000
R/I cost	£525,000
Profit	£975,000

So in a year without big losses his profit is around £1,000,000.

In a year like 1988 the position is:

PI £1,800,000	
Losses in first £150,000	£600,000
R/I cost	£525,000
reinstatement APs	£375,000
Profit	£300,000

He still makes a sizeable profit provided his gross loss does not exceed £4,300,000. Therefore, the reinsurance programme is unsound and too favourable to the reassured. He will be inclined to write for volume. So wait for the next layer of reinsurance or offer to lead a higher layer at a premium no less than these layers.

1995 comment

Agree.

PROPOSITION 28

SLIP DETAILS

REASSURED:	Dingo Insurance Co.
PERIOD:	Losses occurring during 12 months from 1 July 1989.
TYPE:	CATASTROPHE EXCESS OF LOSS COVER (1ST LAYER).
CLASS:	The retained business written by the reinsured in its Domestic & Commercial Sub-divisions (Fire, Car and Allied Perils) including inwards reinsurance written in Reinsurance Division. Excluding: (1) Excess of loss treaty reinsurance. (2) Overeseas reinsurances inwards. (3) Hail insurance on growing and/or standing crop. (4) Sprinkler leakage when written as such. (5) Wind/tornado/cyclone/hurricane when written as such. (6) Liability business.
TERRITORIAL SCOPE:	Australia and incidental exposures in New Zealand.
LIMIT:	A$7,500,000 ultimate net loss each and every loss occurrence excess of A$7,500,000 ultimate net loss each and every loss occurrence.
WARRANTED:	At least two risks be involved in same loss occurrence before recovery hereunder.
REINSTATEMENT:	One reinstatement at 100% a.p. as to time but pro rata amount.
PREMIUM:	Minimum premium A$560,500. deposit premium A$600,000 payable quarterly adjustable at .88% G.N.E.P.I. for 1989 calendar year.
DEDUCTIONS:	Brokerage 10% (nil on reinstatements) plus Australian tax as applicable.
GENERAL CONDITIONS:	Ultimate net loss clause. Net retained lines clause.

War and civil war exclusion.
Nuclear energy risks exclusion reinsurance (1984) NMA 1975.
Extended expiration clause:
72 consecutive hours for earthquake/volcanic eruption
tidal wave/seaquake and or flood.
168 hours for riot, civil commotion and as regards bush fires.
168 hours for any other event of whatsoever nature.

SPECIAL CONDITIONS: (1) Reinsured to be sole judge of what constitutes one risk.

WORDINGS: To be agreed by leading underwriter only.

OTHER LAYERS OFFERED:

		Rate
(2)	A$15,000,000 ×s A$15,000,000	.77% gnpi
(3)	A$45,000,000 ×s A$30,000,000	.72% gnpi
(4)	A$75,000,000 ×s A$75,000,000	.56% gnpi

1989—G.N.E.P.I. A$72,750,000

INFORMATION IN AUSTRALIAN DOLLARS (A$)

(1) Cover

Layer	Limit	Deductible	Rate	A$ Premium	R.O.L.
1	7,500,000	7,500,000	0.88	640,200	8.54%
2	15,000,000	15,000,000	0.77	560,175	3.73%
3	45,000,000	30,000,000	0.72	523,800	1.16%
4	75,000,000	75,000,000	0.56	407,400	0.54%

(2) 89/90 E.P.I. Base

	A$
Commercial Fire	14,550,000
Domestic Fire	52,380,000
Inwards Fac	2,182,500
Inwards TTY Pro rata	3,637,500
TOTAL	72,750,000

(3) 1989 net retained exposures

ZONE	Zone	Net Liability A$	PML	Net PML
Queensland	Brisbane	15,500,000	7.50%	1,162,500
New South Wales	Sydney	15,000,000	2.00%	300,000,000
Western Australia	Perth	26,424,000	7.50%	1,981,800
South Australia	Adelaide	45,361,000	10.00%	4,536,100
Victoria	Melbourne	229,201,136	2.00%	4,584,023

Maximum net retentions

A$7,500,000 any one risk with risks above this figure being protected mainly by Fac excess of loss.

LARGEST LOSSES F.G.U.

	LOSS	AMOUNT
NOV 1976	Storms	2,700,000
FEB 1977	Storms	725,000
MAR 1978	Storms	690,000
1 JUN 1978	Storms	550,000
21 AUG 1981	Storms	500,000
5–9 NOV 1984	Sydney storms	4,400,000
JAN 1986	Orange hail storm	3,000,000
AUG 1986	Sydney storms	5,500,000
OCT 1986	Sydney hail storm	8,300,000
APR 1988	Sydney storms	3,100,000

ASSESSMENT

The layer A$7,500,000 × $7,500,000 would have suffered losses in 1976, 1984 and 1986 on today's 1990 values. The deductible is the same as the risk limit, which could be a first loss retention. A rate of .88 seems thin for an excess at this level.

Ignoring the earthquake risk and other perils, the storm risk with three losses in 15 years must be worth a premium between A$750,000 and A$1,000,000. Decline.

Top excesses

Top layer at rate on line of .54% is way below our minimum of $1½\%/2\%$, so is third layer. So decline whole programme as too cheap.

1995 comment

A wise decision. See proposition 31.

PROPOSITION 29

SLIP DETAILS

REINSURED:	Minisoga Insurance Co.
PERIOD:	12 months losses occurring from 1 April 1991.
TYPE:	FIRST LAYER CATASTROPHE EXCESS OF LOSS.
CLASS:	Japanese business written or accepted by the reinsured in respect of the following classes: All fire policies, Contractors all risks, Burglary, Machinery and erection, Moveables all risks, Glass, Civil engineering risks, Contingency insurance.
TERRITORIAL SCOPE:	Japan.
LIMIT:	To pay up to Yen 900,000,000 each and every loss or series of losses arising out of one event. Excess of: Yen 3,300,000,000 ultimate net loss each and every loss or series of losses arising out of one event.
REINSTATEMENT:	Limited to one full reinstatement at pro rata additional premium.
PREMIUM:	Annual minimum and deposit premium: Yen 50,000,000 payable quarterly in advance, being 1 April 1991, 30 June 1991, 30 September 1991, and 31 December 1991. Adjustable on expiry at 0.1% gross net premium.
DEDUCTIONS:	10% brokerage (Nil for reinstatement).
GENERAL CONDITIONS:	Ultimate net loss clause. Net retained lines clause.
EXCLUSIONS:	(1) Excess of loss reinsurance clause, but excluding excess of loss covers combined with domestic fire quota share treaties of other Japanese companies that exclude earthquake. (2) War exclusion clause.

(3) Nuclear energy risks exclusion clause (reinsurance).
(4) Japanese Government earthquake exclusion clause.

Definition of "each and every loss" per LPO 98A.
(a) 72 consecutive hours as regards a hurricane, a typhoon, windstorm, and/or tornado.
(b) 72 consecutive hours as regards earthquake, seaquake, and/or volcanic eruption.
(c) 72 consecutive hours and within the limits of one city, town or village as regards riots, civil commotions and malicious damage.
(d) 72 consecutive hours as regards any "loss occurrence" that includes individual loss or losses from any of the perils mentioned in (a), (b) and (c).
(e) 168 consecutive hours for any "loss occurrence" of whatsoever nature that does not include individual loss or losses from any of the perils mentioned in (a), (b), and (c) above.

INFORMATION

Synopsis of cover

Yen

Layer	Limit	Deductible	Rate	Premium	R.O.L.
1st	900m	3,300m	0.1	50,883,000	5.7%
2nd	1,800m	4,200m	0.12	61,059,600	3.39%
3rd	1,200m	6,000m	0.05	25,441,500	2.12%

1991/92 premium income base

Yen millions

		1991/92
(a)	Direct Business	
	1. Fire and EC Business	37,504
	2. C.A.R.	1,696
	3. Machinery and Erection	838
	4. Moveables All Risks	6,080
	5. Others	1,584
(b)	Inward Japanese Treaty	
	1. Fire and EC Business	2,466
	2. C.A.R.	203
	3. Machinery and Erection	359
	4. Moveables All Risks	120
	5. Others	

1991/92 premium income base

		Yen millions
(c) Facultative Business		
1. Fire and EC Business		24
2. C.A.R.		0
3. Machinery and Erection		0
		50,883

Catastrophe loss record

		UNL ground up Yen million
1982	Nagasaki storm	230
	Typhoon 18 (flood)	300
1985	Typhoon 13 (windstorm)	900
1986	Typhoon 10 (flood)	600
1987	Typhoon 12 (windstorm)	550
1990	Typhoon 19 (flood)	1,275

Total liabilities for earthquake risks retained for net account

Zone No.	Yen millions At 31/12/90	At 31/12/91
1	1,986.6	2,061.6
2	2,541.6	2,616.6
3	710.4	733.2
4	1,003.2	1,033.2
5	6,363.0	6,567.0
6	5,229.6	5,430.6
7	636.0	660.6
8	3,176.4	3,248.4
9	2,142.0	2,263.8
10	356.4	375.0
11	1,927.8	1,979.4
12	336.6	356.4
	26,409.6	27,325.8

ASSESSMENT

All three layers look thin to me. Of the three I prefer second or third. The third seems remote as it is over four times the 1990 loss and excess of earthquake exposures or nearly so. A small line to help on layer 3 if pressed.

1995 comment

Better to have declined. See proposition 32.

CHAPTER 8

UTOPIAN REINSURANCE 1989-1995

These years were dramatic ones for the worldwide reinsurance markets. They had to contend with enormous increases in past years' reserves for asbestos, pollution and other long-tail claims; in addition a spate of professional indemnity claims from all over the world. In 1989 the property reinsurance market was very competitive and in 1988 and 1989 we declined many catastrophe reinsurances (see Examples 21, 25, 26, 27, 28). The USA had had no major hurricane since 1983 and the international market had had a few significant losses but these were deemed to be exceptional. These included the Windstorm 87J which hit the UK, France and Norway in October 1987, Hurricane Gilbert in 1988 in the Caribbean and the Piper Alpha Rig explosion, also in 1988.

The following years changed that. 1989 had a major USA hurricane (Hugo) which hit the Caribbean and the USA East Coast, also an earthquake in Northern California shortly afterwards. There was a major fire and explosion at Philipp's Petroleum in the USA with losses of over $1,000m and to finish the year an earthquake in Newcastle, Australia.

The market hardened a little after these claims, but what really rocked the market were the European storms in early 1990. A succession of low-pressure systems produced a series of windstorms hitting the United Kingdom, France, Germany and much of Northern Europe. The worst was 90A on 25–26 January and this storm produced insured losses of over $6,000m. The frequency and severity of these windstorms produced substantial losses for reinsurers worldwide and the claims put the nail in the coffin of the LMX, EMX and AMX spirals. These spiral markets had continued to provide retrocessional coverage when there was a decreasing market to retrocede it to. The result was that they had taken substantial commitments on this business and were in fact reinsuring themselves.

Although prices had increased, they were not sufficient to insulate these companies and syndicates from the severe losses. Many syndicates and companies were forced to close in 1990 and the few following years. The spiral market disappeared and at long last the pricing of reinsurance began to return to sensible levels as reinsurers had to retain more and therefore sought higher prices.

The large typhoon Mirielle in 1991 that hit Japan and the large Hurricane Andrew in August 1992 had a further impact on the improvement of terms for reinsurers. They also led to the demise of certain reinsurers worldwide. The year 1993 probably saw the peak of reinsurance rates and they continued in 1994 at a similar level. However, additional capacity was attracted into the market, especially in Bermuda, and this capacity and the good results projected in 1993 and possibly 1994 led to a much more competitive market in 1995.

OUR ADJUSTMENTS TO UNDERWRITING 1989-94

The retrocession programme that we purchased in 1989 and with difficulty in 1990 was severely impacted by Hurricane Hugo and 90A. The reinsurers who had supported us over many years were now in deficit; not hugely, but all the profit built up with them had gone. The pricing of retrocession reinsurance in 1991 increased by over 300% even with an increase in deductibles. Additionally, many of our reinsurers withdrew from the market. Also our surplus treaty, which included treaty catastrophe business, was severely depleted due to the withdrawal of reinsurers.

It was a time for reassessment. In 1991 we had to pay back many of our reinsurers for the deficits they had incurred in 1989 and 1990 and reinsurance costs escalated. However, this was matched by substantial increases in original terms. Many of our clients whom we had reinsured for many years were prepared to pay much higher prices for capacity with good security. We felt it important to try and provide as much capacity as we could without putting our capital at risk. Although we had to reduce some peak exposures, we increased in areas where we were not heavily exposed and where the business was attractively priced. We had to monitor our premium income as we were concerned about our surplus position following poor results in 1989 and 1990. A complete analysis of our portfolio was done. Pro rata business with disappointing results with little future prospect was discarded for commitment to our long-term clients, who needed capacity at much improved terms. The whole process continued in 1992 and in 1993 with the re-engineering of the portfolio.

In 1991, due to the collapse of the retrocessional market we decided to write a balanced net account of LMX and retrocession contracts ourselves. The improvement of information supplied by the reinsurance market to the retrocessionaires allowed us to assess the exposures of reinsurance companies. The production of rate on line profiles on catastrophe business by zone, proper catastrophe aggregates and premium figures assisted us. Additionally, the exclusion of retrocession business and marine, and imposition of two risk warranties, were important. We wrote a spread of business by zone with careful client selection. A strict zone limit of, say, $5,000,000 was set, which would be adjusted dependent on the total premium volume received. The aim was for the zonal limit to be matched by the premium received. The LMX capacity we provided at a critical time gave us goodwill with the brokers so that they showed us other business we wish to underwrite. The venture was successful. The 1991 results produced a 50% profit, 1992 a 30% loss, but 1993 and 1994 were exceptional years with minimal claims.

In 1992, in spite of improved terms, our portfolio was impacted by Hurricane Andrew in Florida. This loss of nearly $20 billion was the largest insured loss to date. The Utopian did not suffer too badly as we had a balanced account with profits elsewhere and our reinsurance helped. We ended up with a small underwriting profit despite Andrew.

The year 1993 offered excellent opportunities; 1992 had been the death knell for some who were overexposed in Florida. Terms and conditions improved significantly and we took advantage of them to expand our business. We also expanded our marine account, which had diminished in the late 1980s and early 1990s as market conditions improved. We also began a credit and surety account following the difficult economic cycle of 1991/92. Our results are encouraging. We have not entered the facultative reinsurance market ourselves, preferring to support specialist facultative underwriters elsewhere.

As we have grown we have needed to recruit more employees. We now have a small team of underwriters who have specialist areas, but they all report daily to the main underwriter and each other.

PLAN FOR 1995

Our net capacity per property programme is now $3,000,000; $5,000,000 with our surplus. We aim to continue to be an important part of the market.

The year 1995 will be more competitive. We will support our long-term clients. We may let business go if it becomes too competitive. We will continue to look for new opportunities. Our philosophy will not change.

PROPOSITION 30

SLIP DETAILS

REASSURED:	Bald Eagle Insurance Company.
PERIOD:	12 months losses occurring from 1 April 1994.
TYPE:	CATASTROPHE EXCESS COVER (3RD LAYER).
CLASS:	Covering all business classified by the reassured as property including, but not limited to, Homeowners & Farmowners multi-peril and commercial multi-peril, Boiler & Machinery, Glass, Ocean & Inland Marine, and Commercial. Automobile Physical Damage.
TERRITORIAL SCOPE:	Anywhere in the USA and Canada.
LIMIT:	To pay up to $25,000,000 each and every loss occurrence excess of $80,000,000 ultimate net loss each and every loss occurrence.
WARRANTY:	Reassured to retain 10% hereon net and unreinsured.
REINSTATEMENT:	One reinstatement at 100% a.p. as to time but pro rata as to amount.
PREMIUM:	Minimum Premium / Deposit Premium $5,000,000 payable quarterly adjustable at .63% G.N.E.P.I. for 1994 calendar year.
DEDUCTIONS:	Brokerage 10%.
EXCLUSIONS:	1. Loss to growing and standing timber. 2. Ordinary and group life insurance. 3. Financial guarantee and insolvency. 4. War risks as per wordings. 5. Insolvency funds exclusion. 6. Nuclear exclusion clause. 7. All surety bonds. 8. As respects property—business excluded by the pools association and syndicate exclusion clause. 9. Occupational disease. 10. Seepage and pollution exclusion clause.

Proposition 30

	11. Workers' compensation/employers' liability.
	12. Extra contractual obligation as per wording.
GENERAL CONDITIONS:	Ultimate net loss clause, including loss expenses & costs.
	Net retained lines clause.
	Extended expiration clause.
	72 hours for wind & riot.
	168 hours for earthquake, freeze & all other property perils.
	Service of suit clause.
	Currency clause.
	Insolvency clause.
	Mediation clause.
	Arbitration clause.
	Access to records.
	Reinsurance tax clause.
	Self-insured obligations clause.
	Indemnifications and errors and omissions clause.
OTHER LAYERS OFFERED:	1. $15,000,000 × $45,000,000 .635 gnpi.
	2. $20,000,000 × $60,000,000 .69% gnpi.
	All with 10% co-reinsurance.
	1994—G.N.E.P.I. $840,000,000.

INFORMATION

Synopsis of cover in millions of US$

Layer	Limit	Deductible	Rate	$ Premium	ROL
1	$15	$45	.635	5.33	35.5%
2	$20	$60	.69	5.80	29.0%
3	$25	$80	.62	5.20	20.6%

1 Reinstatement at 100% on all layers

94/95 EPI Base in millions of US$

	$
Homeowners	240
Inland Marine	50
Auto Physical Damage ex Collision	200
Commercial Multi-peril	250
Commercial Fire	100
TOTAL	840

1994 California E/Q Aggs in millions of US$

Area	Zone	Net Liability	Net PML
San Francisco	A	1,100	550
L.A./Orange County	B	1,350	190
Santa Barbara	C	205	15
San Diego	D	175	40
South East	E	500	42
Central	F	80	22
North Central	G	120	40
North	H	7	3

Catastrophe losses

Greater than $20,000,000		In millions
Alicia – 15	17–20/8/83	25.0
Gloria – 82	25/9/85	15.5
Hugo – 18	21–22/9/89	47.0
Winter freeze – 24	21–26/12/89	16.0
Hail – 89	3–6/5/89	12.0
Loma Prieta E/Q – 20	17/10/89	14.0
Bob – 85	18/9/91	11.0
Andrew – 27	24/8/92	106.0
Northridge E/Q	17/1/94	62.5

EPI breakdown by States

	Market share		Market share
North East	6.70%	**Atlantic States**	3.25%
Connecticut	8.60%	Pennsylvania	5.60%
New York	7.20%	Virginia	4.15%
Rhode Is.	5.90%	New Jersey	2.78%
Massachusetts	4.90%	Delaware	2.34%
Utah	3.00%		
New Hampshire	2.10%	**Carolinas & Georgia**	1.90%
Maine	1.45%	North Carolina	3.20%
		South Carolina	1.35%
South East	2.20%	Georgia	1.06%
Florida	2.56%		
Louisiana	2.10%	California	2.07%
Alabama	1.76%	Texas	2.14%
Mississippi	1.41%	Others	16.85%

Proposition 30

BALD EAGLE

Comment

This programme was one we looked at in 1989 (Proposition 24) and the assessment made there is worth looking at now as the programme was severely affected by Hurricane Hugo and, more importantly, hit by Hurricane Andrew in 1992 ($106m).

A quick comparison for 1989 to 1994 is worthy of merit.

	1989	ROL	1994	ROL
	12.5 × 40	18.0%	15m × 45m	35.5%
	15.0 × 52.5	12.2%	20m × 60m	29.1%
	15.0 × 67.5	9.4%	25m × 80m	20.6%
	17.5 × 82.5	6.75%		
	30 × 100	5.0%		
Ex Comp Income	$660m		$840m	

Even allowing for inflation and growth in income, the pricing of the layers is greatly improved and the immediate temptation is to take increased participations. However, we must make sure there are no other significant changes.

Therefore, we ask the broker: Have there been any changes to underwriting guidelines, reinsurance protections or business written that would have either improved or deteriorated the Andrew or Northridge losses.

Response:

The company in 1992 had two surplus treaties, a risk excess and they used facultative reinsurance extensively. The gross and net losses inuring to reinsurances are shown:

		Andrew loss		Northridge loss
	1992		1994	
Surplus 1	$20m	$65m	Surplus $20m	$30m
Surplus 2	$15m	$25m		
Risk XL	$20m	$40m	Risk XL $15m	$20m
Net Retn	$12.5m	$106m	$15m	$62.5m
Fac Above	$67.5m	$35m	$50m	$11m
Gross		$266m		$123.5m
Automatic Capacity		$67.5m		$50m

After 1992 the company dropped the second surplus due to poor results and a $50m occurrence limit was incorporated in the treaty. For 1992 and 1994 the risk excess had an occurrence limit of twice the risk limit ($40m in 1992, $30m in 1994).

The company has reduced down its line size on earthquake in California from $40m per risk to $30m gross since Northridge. They have also reduced their commercial business in Florida by 15% since 1992. Note, however, much of their exposure is homeowners, say 10% reduction overall.

As if Gross Andrew Loss, say $266m × 0.9 = $239m
Less 50m surplus, 30m risk and say 25m fac = 134m.

Therefore the "as if" net loss has actually gone up!

ASSESSMENT

Since we assessed the programme in 1989 there have been changes in the portfolio. The Homeowners income has fallen from $260m to $240m, which is a real reduction in market share. The Inland Marine & Commercial account combined has increased from $280m to $405m, which is a considerable increase. During this period rates have remained pretty stable, so this represents an exposure increase. If we say the catastrophe factor on the Homeowners account in 1989 is 75% and on the Commercial account (25%), then the Catastrophe content of premium base for 1989 would be $(260 \times 0.75 + 280 \times 0.25) = 265$ and 1995 would be $(240 \times 0.75 + 405 \times 0.25) = 281$. This represents an increase of 281/265 or 9%.

Earthquake

The Northridge earthquake was a good illustration of what could happen but it was a relatively modest earthquake: 6.8 on the Richter scale. It must be noted, however, that due to the high vertical movement of the earthquake (most earthquakes have mainly horizontal movement) the damage done was much greater than a normal quake of this magnitude. The market insured loss is now $12 billion! This programme was quoted soon after the quake and their loss was $62.5m. However, due to late reporting of claims we would expect the loss to rise to say $80m. The inuring reinsurance programme is the same as last year so the same earthquake happening again would result in a similar loss. I would expect some tightening of underwriting guidelines, but the lack of facultative capacity would probably mean a similar net loss.

The whole programme is exposed to earthquake in California and also probably in New Madrid and in Washington. The price for earthquake reinsurance is higher than in 1989 due to lack of retrocession capacity and the realisation that the product was underpriced.

Please note that WCA is no longer covered so there is a reduction of exposure there.

Windstorm

Hurricane Andrew is a good illustration of what could happen but it could have been worse. If the hurricane had been 50 miles further north the market loss could have been $50bn rather than the $20bn insured loss. The other major exposure to this company is New York and New England where a $30bn hurricane loss could easily be foreseen.

The past "as if" losses could be:

	Actual loss			**As if loss**
Frederick	$10m	×4	=	$40m
Alicia	$26m	×3	=	$78m
Elena	$10m	×2.5	=	$25m
Gloria	15m	×2.5	=	$37.5m
Hugo	$47m	×1.5	=	$70.5m
Andrew	$106m			$134m
Northridge	$80m			$80m

Using these "as if" losses above the burning cost of layers would be:

Layers	5 Yr Losses	ROL	10 Yr Losses	ROL	20 Yr Losses	ROL	Act Price
15 × 45	45	60%	45	30%	60	20%	35.5%
20 × 60	50.5	50.5%	50.5	25.5%	68.5	17.1%	29.1%
25 × 80	25	20%	25	10%	25	5%	20.6%

The above Rate on Lines (ROL) ignore the reinstatement premiums and also costs.

In view of reinstatements of 1 @ 100% all layers look attractive, bearing in mind brokerage at 15% and own costs of, say, 7.5%. It is worth giving more emphasis to 10 year burning cost rather than five years as the five-year record is exceptional. On lower layers the five-year record may be more appropriate but on higher layers a 20-year or greater record is more sensible.

The first layer is exposed to most of the same events as the second layer but we would prefer to have the extra deductible even though there is a slightly lower price. The top layer in 1989 was only partly affected by Andrew and there is no historical deficit; the 20 year burning cost is well below the price and we will offer a meaningful line on this layer.

Therefore second layer we offer 4% = $600,000.

Top layer we offer a meaningful line of 10% = or $2,500,000. See proposition 24.

PROPOSITION 31

SLIP DETAILS

REASSURED:	Dingo Insurance Co.
PERIOD:	Losses occurring during 12 months from 1 July 1994.
TYPE:	CATASTROPHE EXCESS OF LOSS COVER (1ST LAYER).
CLASS:	The retained business written by the reinsured classified as Domestic and Commercial (Fire, Car and Allied Perils) including inwards Facultative. Excluding: (1) Inwards reinsurance other than facultative. (2) Hail insurance on growing and/or standing crop. (3) Sprinkler leakage when written as such. (4) Wind/tornado/cyclone/hurricane when written as such. (5) Special personal effects insurance (previously all risks). (6) Pluvius insurances. (7) Liability business.
TERRITORIAL SCOPE:	Australia and incidental exposures in New Zealand.
LIMIT:	A$30,000,000 ultimate net loss each and every loss occurrence excess of A$20,000,000 ultimate net loss each and every loss occurrence.
CO-REINSURANCE WARRANTED:	10% retained net and unreinsured.
REINSTATEMENT:	One reinstatement at 100% a.p. as to time but pro rata amount.
PREMIUM:	Minimum Premium A$6,000,000 Deposit Premium A$6,750,000 payable quarterly adjustable at 5.15% G.N.E.P.I. for 1994 calendar year.
DEDUCTIONS:	Brokerage 10% (nil on reinstatements) plus Australian tax as applicable.
GENERAL CONDITIONS:	Ultimate net loss clause. Net retained lines clause. War and civil war exclusion.

Nuclear energy risks exclusion reinsurance (1984) NMA 1975.
Extended expiration clause:
72 consecutive hours for earthquake/volcanic eruption
tidal wave/seaquake and or flood.
168 hours for riot, civil commotion and as regards bush fires.
168 hours for any other event of whatsoever nature.
Transmission and distribution lines exclusion.
Reinsurance to be subject to law and jurisdiction of N.S.W.
Seat of arbitration: Sydney, Australia.

SPECIAL CONDITIONS:
(1) Reinsured to be sole judge of what constitutes one risk.
(2) In the event of one loss occurrence giving rise to a claim to this agreement in respect of two or more of the reinsured's insurance subsidiaries, the limit and deductible shall be applied to the aggregate of all such losses from the same loss occurrence.

WORDINGS: To be agreed by leading underwriter only.

OTHER LAYERS OFFERED:

		Rate
(2)	A$50,000,000 xs A$50,000,000	5.15% gnpi
(3)	A$75,000,000 xs A$100,000,000	3.95% gnpi
(4)	A$150,000,000 xs A$175,000,000	3.66 gnpi

1994/95 – G.N.E.P.I. A$131,000,000

Maximum net retentions

A$12,500,000 any one risk.

Largest losses F.G.U. in A$

	Loss	Amount
5–9 November 1984	Sydney storms	5,000,000
January 1986	Orange hail storm	3,500,000
August 1986	Sydney storms	6,000,000
October 1986	Sydney hail storm	7,750,000
December 1989	Newcastle earthquake	105,000,000
March 1990	Sydney hail storm	27,000,000
January 1991	Sydney storms	15,000,000
12 February 1992	Western Sydney hail storms	3,500,000
6 October	N.S.W. Bushfires	9,000,000

1994 net retained exposures in millions of A$

State	Main zone	Net liability	PML	Net PML
Queensland	Brisbane	2,500	7.50%	187.5
New South Wales	Sydney	25,000	2.00%	500
Western Australia	Perth	1,500	7.50%	112.5
South Australia	Adelaide	625	10.00%	62.5
Victoria	Melbourne	8,100	2.00%	162

INFORMATION IN AUSTRALIAN DOLLARS (A$)

(1) Synopsis of cover

Layer	Limit	Deductible	Rate	A$ premium	ROL
1	30,000,000	20,000,000	5.15	6,750,000	22.5%
2	50,000,000	50,000,000	5.15	6,750,000	13.5%
3	75,000,000	100,000,000	3.95	5,175,000	6.9%
4	150,000,000	175,000,000	3.66	4,800,000	3.2%

(2) 94/95 EPI base

	A$
Householders	104,000,000
Commercial	27,000,000
Total	131,000,000

(3) Percentage split of estimated gross written net premium income by State 1994/95

	Householders	Commercial
Queensland	10%	5%
New South Wales	65%	70%
Victoria	20%	15%
Southern Australia	2%	5%
Western Australia	3%	5%
Total	100%	100%

DINGO INSURANCE

The Dingo Insurance Company is one programme we looked at in 1989 (Proposition 28) and declined, thus we avoided the Newcastle earthquake loss. We were able to get on this programme in 1991 due to lack of market capacity and we benefited from the improvement in pricing.

In the Newcastle earthquake, although the earthquake was only 5.4 on the Richter scale, the market loss was about A$1,000m. Most companies lost 5% of the sums insured in the Newcastle zone. The deductibles on Australian household policies were minimal and the old masonry construction was prone to damage.

ASSESSMENT

Main earthquake exposures are in Perth and Adelaide or some unexpected place like Newcastle. Australia is a relatively inactive area for earthquake but as the deductibles (excesses) are so low a loss of 10% of sums insured in Adelaide or Perth is possible; a loss of 2.5% in Sydney is possible also.

Australia is also prone to bushfires such as the one in 1983 and as there is a 168 hours clause nationwide they could affect a wide area.

Hailstorm is an exposure in suburban areas such as Brisbane and Sydney.

Cyclone is a hazard on the Queensland coast and in the Northern Territories and Western Australia.

My assessment of prices in rate on line on various layers is as follows:

Layer	Bushfire	Earthquake	Cyclone	Hailstorm	Flood	Total
1	5%	4%	10%	2%	2%	23%
2	1%	3%	7.5%	1%	1%	13.5%
3	0.5%	2%	4%			6.5%
4		1.5%	2%			3.5%

These compare remarkably well with what the programme is paying and in view of the reinstatement premiums we would support the programme with modest lines.

The top layer in view of the stretch is worth good support and the first layer in view of reinstatement terms. Therefore we would offer:

	A$	A$
2% on 1st layer of	30,000,000 =	600,000
3% on 2nd layer of	50,000,000 =	1,500,000
2% on top layer of	150,000,000 =	3,000,000

A total in Sterling of £2,550,000

This would give us a major commitment and we will make cessions to our surplus treaty. We have a good relationship with client and have other lines of business with them.

PROPOSITION 32

SLIP DETAILS

REINSURED:	Minisoga Insurance Co.
PERIOD:	12 months losses occurring from 1 April 1994.
TYPE:	FIRST LAYER CATASTROPHE EXCESS OF LOSS.
CLASS:	Japanese business written or accepted by the reinsured in respect of the following classes: All fire policies, Contractors all risks, Burglary, Machinery and erection, Moveables all risks, Glass, Civil engineering risks, Contingency insurance.
TERRITORIAL SCOPE:	Japan.
LIMIT:	To pay up to Yen 3,900,000,000 each and every loss or series of losses arising out of one event. Excess of: Yen 6,300,000,000 ultimate net loss each and every loss or series of losses arising out of one event.
REINSTATEMENT:	Limited to one full reinstatement at pro rata additional premium calculated pro rata to amount, 100% to time.
PREMIUM:	Annual minimum and deposit premium: Yen 821,749,050 payable half yearly in advance. Adjustable on expiry at 1.62% gross net premium income.
DEDUCTIONS:	10% brokerage (Nil for reinstatement).
GENERAL CONDITIONS:	Ultimate net loss clause. Net retained lines clause.
EXCLUSIONS:	(1) Excess of loss reinsurance clause, but excluding excess of loss covers combined with domestic fire quota share treaties of other Japanese companies that exclude earthquake. (2) War exclusion clause. (3) Nuclear energy risks exclusion clause (reinsurance). (4) Excluding overhead transmission and distribution lines except for NTT and JR East policies.

Definition of "each and every loss" per LP098A:
(a) 72 consecutive hours as regards a hurricane, a typhoon, windstorm, and/or tornado.
(b) 168 consecutive hours for any "loss occurrence" of whatsoever nature which does not include individual loss or losses from any of the perils mentioned in (a), (b), and (c) above.

INFORMATION

Synopsis of cover

Yen

Layer	Limit	Deductible	Rate	Premium	ROL
1st	3,900m	6,300m	1.62	864,999,000	22.2%
2nd	4,200m	10,200m	1.3	694,135,000	16.53%
3rd	5,400m	14,400m	1.2	640,740,000	11.87%
4th	4,200m	19,800m	0.7	373,765,000	8.90%

1994/95 premium income base

Estimated Gross Net Premium Income

		Yen millions 1994/95
(a) Direct Business		
	1. Fire and EC Business	40,879
	2. C.A.R.	1,600
	3. Machinery and Erection	670
	4. Moveables All Risks	7,073
	5. Others	205
(b) Inward Japanese Treaty		
	1. Fire and EC Business	2,410
	2. C.A.R.	114
	3. Machinery and Erection	267
	4. Moveables All Risks	154
	5. Others	0
(c) Facultative Business		
	1. Fire and EC Business	24
	2. C.A.R.	0
	3. Machinery and Erection	0
		53,395

Catastrophe loss record

		UNL ground up Yen million
1982	Nagasaki storm	226
	Typhoon 18 (flood)	319
1985	Typhoon 13 (windstorm)	900
1986	Typhoon 10 (flood)	592
1987	Typhoon 12 (windstorm)	563
1990	Typhoon 19 (flood)	1,286
1991	Typhoon 17 (flood)	1,772
	Typhoon 19 (windstorm)	20,709
1992	Typhoon 10	1,074

MINISOGA

We supported the Minisoga programme in 1991 (Proposition 29) for a small line and were affected by the typhoon that struck Japan that August. This typhoon produced a market insured loss of over $6,000m.

We had miscalculated the size of a potential loss to hit Japan, so had the Japanese companies. The companies in general lost between 30% and 50% of their Property programme income in the typhoon or 0.1% of their sums insured—very similar to what UK companies lost in 90A in 1990.

Following the loss the pricing on the catastrophe programmes increased significantly and now they seem well priced.

It is difficult to assess the likelihood of the loss without historical data and this is sketchy due to little insurance coverage for wind before the mid-1980s in Japan, and also the growth in values and construction. The major cyclones to hit Japan were Vera in 1959 and one in 1961. It is difficult to assess the "as if" loss for Typhoon Mirielle, but we would expect it to total the programme. The differential in pricing between the layers seems fair but the reinstatement premiums are @ 100% throughout so we would favour the lower layers. We would offer to do 2% on the lower two layers and 1% on the top two.

We could do more but it is linked to what we do on other business with the company and also our loss on Mirielle.

PROPOSITION 33

SLIP DETAILS

REINSURED:	Nautilus. Insurance Company.
TYPE:	75% OBLIGATORY QUOTA SHARE TREATY.
TO COVER:	Insurance of off-shore and on-shore oil and/or gas and/or other extractive businesses and similar or affiliated properties including but not limited to drilling rigs, platforms, barges, vessels, cost of control, drilling equipment and supplies, liabilities, removal of debris, contractual liability associated with this class of business and such other insurances as are normally required by companies engaged in oil and/or gas and/or other extraction, exploration, production or development written anywhere in the world.
EXCLUSIONS:	1. (A) Reinsurance treaty business, except business offered by captives or similar schemes considered as if written directly. 　(B) London Market excess of loss written on an "Automatic" facultative and/or treaty basis. 2. Confiscation, Expropriation, Nationalisation, and Deprivation unless the original insurance is in accordance with one of the Standard War and/or SRCC Clauses and/or Terrorist Risk Clauses. 3. Business interruption or third party liability risks insured on a "stand alone" basis. 4. Performance bonds and guarantee risks. 5. (A) Premium Swing Protection Policies. 　(B) Deductible Buyback Policies. It is understood and agreed that this exclusion does not apply to policies comprising individual risks that lie entirely or substantially beneath the O.I.L. Policy attachment point, AND provided that such risks are individually underwritten and rated.
GEOGRAPHICAL SCOPE:	Worldwide.
PREMIUM:	1. On original contracts written as direct insurance, the commission shall be the original acquisition costs including commissions, dis-

counts, brokerage, taxes and any other expenses paid by the reinsured on the original net premiums (being net of all return premiums and all other reinsurance premiums) plus a further 7.5% applied on original gross premiums.

2. On original contracts written as facultative reinsurance the commission shall be the original acquisition costs including commissions, discounts, brokerage, taxes and any other expenses paid by the reinsured on the original net premiums (being net of all return premiums and all other reinsurance premiums) plus a further 5% applied on original gross premiums.

Over all contracts the commission allowance shall not exceed 30%.

BROKERAGE:	2.50% on net.
PROFIT COMMISSION:	10% payable at the end of the third year with 7.50% reinsurance expense allowance. Six-year deficit carry forward.
ACCOUNTS:	Quarterly.
CASH LOSS CLAUSE:	US$1,000,000.
TAX:	1.00% Federal Excise Tax payable if and as applicable.
WORDING:	To be agreed L/U only.
PERIOD:	Continuous at 1 January 1995 subject to 90 days advance cancellation notice prior to 1 January each year. Maximum period for any one risk shall be 12 months plus odd time (not to exceed 18 months in total).
LIMIT:	US$12,500,000 any one risk or any one platform or structure. It is understood and agreed that the treaty limit is a combined single limit applicable to the insured value in respect of any one risk. A risk shall mean any one assured and/or any one platform or structure, for all assureds, all policies and coverages combined, regardless of the underwriting year to which different policies covering the same risk might attach.

In the event the risk limit is in excess of the agreed treaty limit involving more than one policy year, the treaty limit for each policy year shall be the ratio of the risk limit attaching in that policy year to the total risk limit attaching, multiplied by the treaty limit.

Offshore facilities rigidly interconnected (otherwise than by pipelines only) are considered to be one risk.

Reinsurers shall not be liable in the excess of the above combined single limit in respect of any one risk for all losses arising out of one and the same event or occurrence.

When insured on a stand alone basis, without benefit of the basic Physical Damage/Hull coverage, cessions in respect of the following interests shall be limited to a maximum of US$1,500,000 per risk:
- Increased Value
- Loss of Hire
- Stores and Bunkers
- Sue and Labour
- Removal of Wreck/Debris

RETENTION: Minimum retention 25%.

CONDITIONS: Subject to all terms, clauses, conditions as per original policy(ies) and to follow the original in every respect, liable or not liable.
Non-admitted reinsurance clause, if applicable.
Extra contractual obligations inclusion clause. (For a separate and additional limit.)
War inclusion clause.
Institute radioactive contamination exclusion clause.
Nuclear energy risks exclusion clause 1 January 1989.
Refinery exclusion clause 1993 (REC 1993).

> It is understood and agreed that those properties not excluded under "REC 1993" and/or those non-marine liabilities in accordance with "SPEC" and "LEC B" may be written but the maximum cession to the treaty shall be limited to US$2,500,000 combined single limit over such properties and/or non-marine liability risks.

Non-marine liability exclusion clause "B".
Seepage and pollution exclusion clause.
Special termination or settlement clause.
Access to records clause.
Error and omission clause.
Arbitration clause.
Loss and loss adjustment expense clause.

COMMENTS

1. The company is a worldwide group which specialises in marine business.
2. They began writing oil rig business in the early 1980s and started a quota share treaty in 1988 to give them more capacity. They have specialist teams based both in London and in the USA. They have their own team of engineers but do contract out some inspections, etc., in remote locations.
3. The company expanded the account following the major market losses of Piper Alpha and Enchova. However, more competition has returned to the market-place and also some oil companies are insuring less. Therefore, they expect the premium income to fall in 1995.

ASSESSMENT

4. The company has a very good record through the difficult years of 1988 to 1990. They also expanded when market conditions improved in 1991 and 1992.
5. This quota share has minimal on-shore exposure and non-marine liability. These conditions were tightened in 1990 and 1991.
6. The loss development looks stable with only 1989 showing a late deterioration and this is modest. The treaty is on a risks attaching basis and therefore it will take maybe 30 months before all losses are known.
7. The balance of the treaty looks reasonable on a per rig basis. However, there will be accumulations in the North Sea and Caribbean. The peak exposures in one zone according to insured are US$60,000,000 in the North Sea and US$20,000,000 in the Caribbean. The PML in the Caribbean we could assume to be US$20,000,000 their zone limit. However, the likelihood of a major event in the North Sea that would affect many oil rigs is small. They are built to withstand high winds and waves. Potentially a seaquake or a fire conflagration are possibilities. I would assess the PML as two total rigs, i.e. US$25,000,000.
8. This treaty shows the classic plus points of expansion in a hard market and contraction in a soft market. The company is a specialist and will probably outperform the dabbling market. The commissions averaging 25% look reasonable and profit commission is modest. My assessment is we should take a participation as this seems a sound

proposition and our exposure on this class is low. There is also little clash with other accounts and long-tail exposure is minimal. I would offer a line of 2.5% which would give us a premium of US$450,000 a limit per rig of US$312,500 and US$500,000 PML. This could be increased to a maximum of 5% if we met the underwriting team and we were entirely happy with their underwriting and catastrophe control.

NAUTILUS RIG QUOTA SHARE

(Figures in thousands of US$)

Nautilus Ins Co Oil Rig Q/s

Year	Written premium	Earned premium	Comm'n	Premium balance	Paid claims	o/s claims	Incurred claims	Inc'd %	Profit (loss)
1988	4,500	4,500	1,125	3,375	2,050	150	2,200	49%	1,175
1989	8,500	8,500	2,125	6,375	7,250	200	7,450	88%	−1,075
1990	17,250	17,250	4,313	12,938	9,150	2,200	11,350	66%	1,588
1991	28,000	28,000	6,720	21,280	13,100	3,750	16,850	60%	4,430
1992	30,000	29,700	7,200	22,800	5,250	2,600	7,850	26%	14,950
1993	26,250	20,000	6,300	19,950	1,500	2,625	4,125	16%	15,825
1994	10,000	3,000	2,400	7,600	0	0	0	0%	7,600
Total	124,500	110,950	30,183	94,318	38,300	11,525	49,825	40%	44,493

Premium projected

1994 22,000
1995 18,000

Max rig line

12,500.

Loss record

		US$ m	
1988	Piper Alpha	1,250	
1990	Advent Petroleum	5,000	
1991/92	Hurricane Andrew	12,500	1991 year
		2,500	1992 year
1993	New Zealand Gas	2,200	

Development of incurred loss ratios in percentages calculated from brokers accounts

Months	1988	1989	1990	1991	1992	1993	1994
6	20	5	10	25	25	9.4	0
18	65	60	35	20	75	15.7	
30	55	85	70	62.2	26.1		
42	50	83	67.3	60.1			
54	49.5	85	65.7				
66	48	87.6					
78	48.9						

PROPOSITION 34

SLIP DETAILS

REASSURED:	Pall Mall Insurance Company.
PERIOD:	Losses occurring during 12 months at 1 January 1996.
TYPE:	EXCESS OF LOSS.
CLASS:	Motor including Green Card cover.
LIMIT:	£500,000 each and every accident. Excess of: £500,000 each and every accident.
PREMIUM:	Minimum and Deposit premium £475,000 payable in advance, adjustable on expiry at 1.22% of the reassured's original net premium income accounted for during the period of this reinsurance.
DEDUCTIONS:	10%.
TERRITORIAL SCOPE:	Business underwritten in the United Kingdom.
GENERAL CONDITIONS:	Net retained lines clause. Ultimate net loss clause. War and civil war exclusion clause. Nuclear energy risks exclusion clause (reinsurance) (1994)—NMA 1975a. Portfolio run-off clause at terms to be agreed by leading underwriter. London Market index clause. Base date 1.1.95 (fully indexed). Reassured to have the benefit of recoveries on underlying reinsurances, with allowance for indexed annuities. Warranted original third party property damage limit for commercial vehicles £5,000,000. Change in law clause. Claims co-operation clause. *Several Liability Notice—LSW 1001 (Reinsurance)* The subscribing reinsurers' obligations under contracts of reinsurance to which they subscribe are several and not joint and are limited solely to the extent of their individual subscriptions. The subscribing reinsurers are not responsible for the subscription of any co-subscribing reinsurer who for any reason does not satisfy all or part of its obligations.

WORDING:	Special acceptance as before as far as applicable, or to be agreed by leading underwriter only.
INFORMATION:	Estimated original net premium income: 1995 £43,500,000. 1996 £45,000,000.
OTHER LAYERS:	£1,000,000 xs £1,000,000 Rate 0.777% MDP 300,000 payable half yearly.
	£3,000,000 xs £2,000,000 Rate 0.422% MDP 160,000 payable half yearly. Own damage losses limited to £1,000,000 hereon with one free reinstatement.
	£5,000,000 xs £5,000,000 Rate 0.185% MDP 75,000. Own damage losses excluded.
	Unlimited xs £10,000,000 Rate 0.422% MDP 160,000 payable inception. Own damage losses excluded.

PREMIUMS

Pall Mall Insurance

Premium income £'000					Our policy increase factor
	Agents	Direct	Total	Vehicle no	
1986	2,750		2,750	18,100	1000.0%
1987	4,250		4,250	22,625	800.0%
1988	5,100		5,100	28,400	637.3%
1989	6,250		6,250	31,250	579.2%
1990	8,100		8,100	42,631	424.6%
1991	9,500		9,500	52,770	343.0%
1992	10,750	1,250	12,000	59,722	303.1%
1993	12,500	6,500	19,000	73,255	247.1%
1994	17,500	12,500	30,000	121,054	149.5%
1995	22,500	21,000	43,500	172,152	105.1%
1996	21,500	23,500	45,000	181,000	100.0%

Mix of portfolio

90% comprehensive, 10% third party fire & theft only.
90% private cars, 5% commercial vehicles,
2% self drive cars, 1% minibuses.

LOSS HISTORY

Pall Mall loss history (All losses above £100,000 in £'000)

		1 yr	2 yr	3 yr	4 yr	5 yr	6 yr	7 yr	8 yr	9 yr	Claim status	Current loss
1986	1	0	200	225	240	330s						330
	2	0	150	200	230	230	175s					175
	3	50	150	175	175	250	300	350	725s			725
1987	1	100	125	125	105s							105
	2	0	0	250	300s							300
	3	150	200	400	350	325	350	350	350	400	o/s	400
	4	0	0	0	50	200s						200
1988	1	75	100	200	205	250	275s					275
	2	100	250	250	350	350	400	425	425		o/s	425
	3	0	200	150s								150
1989	1	100	125	115s								115
	2	50	50	50	200	212s						212
	3	0	0	250	275	275	300	300			o/s	300
	4	0	0	0	225	250	275	275			o/s	275
	5	350	400	275s								275
	6	50	250	400	800	850	850	950			o/s	950
	7	0	100	150	225	232s						232
1990	1	100	125	175	250	242s						242
	2	0	75	150	195	237s						237
	3	0	0	0	150	350	375				o/s	375
	4	0	200	400	355s							355
	5	0	0	0	100	175	175				o/s	175
	6	0	0	0	200	265s						265
	7	0	0	150	175s							175
	8	0	150	206s								206
	9	0	0	0	250	350	325				o/s	325
	10	0	0	0	50	150	150				o/s	150
1991	1	125	250	400	400	450					o/s	450
	2	0	0	0	325	350					o/s	350
	3	100	125	227s								227
	4	0	0	0	150	150					o/s	150
	5	100	100	125	125	125					o/s	125
	6	300	325	316s								316
	7	0	0	175	200s							200
	8	0	0	0	250	250					o/s	250
1992	1	100	225	251s								251
	2	250	250	250	250						o/s	250
	3	0	0	250	500						o/s	500
	4	0	0	187s								187
	5	95	150	150	175						o/s	175
	6	0	150	200	200						o/s	200
	7	0	0	125	150						o/s	150

		1 yr	2 yr	3 yr	4 yr	5 yr	6 yr	7 yr	8 yr	9 yr	Claim status	Current loss
1993	1	150	210s									210
	2	0	150	150							o/s	150
	3	0	150	150							o/s	150
	4	0	200	250							o/s	250
	5	0	350	350							o/s	350
	6	100	200	225							o/s	225
	7	0	0	300							o/s	300
1994	1	100	150								o/s	150
	2	150	200								o/s	200
	3	125	111s									111
	4	200	195s									195
	5	0	350								o/s	350
	6	0	175								o/s	175
	7	0	300								o/s	300
1995											o/s	200
	1	200									o/s	250
	2	250									o/s	150
	3	150										

LOSS COST (OUR FIGURES)

A		Loss cost with 10% indexation per annum				
	Limit Excess	£500,000 £500,000	£1,000,000 £1,000,000	£3,000,000 £2,000,000	£5,000,000 £5,000,000	unlimited £10,000,000
1986		£856,000	£880,000			
1987		£697,000				
1988		£589,000	£2,000			
1989		£881,000	£1,000,000	£222,000		
1990		£741,000				
1991		£911,000	£51,000			
1992		£586,000	£171,000			
1993		£620,000				
1994		£573,000				
1995		£119,000				
B		Loss cost as "A" above multiplied by policy count increase				
	Policy count Increase	£500,000 £500,000	£1,000,000 £1,000,000	£3,000,000 £2,000,000	£5,000,000 £5,000,000	unlimited £10,000,000
1986	1000%	£8,560,000	£8,800,000	£0	£0	£0
1987	800%	£5,576,000	£0	£0	£0	£0
1988	637%	£3,751,930	£12,740	£0	£0	£0
1989	579%	£5,100,990	£5,790,000	£1,285,380	£0	£0
1990	425%	£3,149,250	£0	£0	£0	£0
1991	343%	£3,124,730	£174,930	£0	£0	£0
1992	303%	£1,775,580	£518,130	£0	£0	£0
1993	247%	£1,531,400	£0	£0	£0	£0
1994	149%	£853,770	£0	£0	£0	£0
1995	105%	£124,950	£0	£0	£0	£0

C		Loss cost as "B" above multiplied by IBNR factor				
	IBNR factor	£500,000 £500,000	£1,000,000 £1,000,000	£3,000,000 £2,000,000	£5,000,000 £5,000,000	unlimited £10,000,000
1986	100%	£8,560,000	£8,800,000	£0		
1987	100%	£5,576,000	£0	£0		
1988	100%	£3,751,930	£12,740	£0		
1989	100%	£5,100,990	£5,790,000	£1,285,380		
1990	100%	£3,149,250	£192,423	£0		
1991	110%	£3,437,203	£192,423	£0		
1992	125%	£2,219,475	£647,663	£0		
1993	150%	£2,297,100	£0	£0		
1994	200%	£1,707,540	£0	£0		
1995	300%	£374,850	£0	£0		
Average annual cost		£3,617,000	£1,544,000	£129,000		
Offered premium		£550,000	£350,000	£190,000	£83,000	£190,000
Decision		decline	decline	decline	accept	accept

PALL MALL INSURANCE

Comments

This is a motor XL programme covering UK insureds while driving in the United Kingdom or on green cards abroad. The cover has unlimited reinstatements so there is no limitation on the maximum that can be paid on the contract. Additionally, the top layer is an unlimited layer with no vertical limit either. The whole programme is indexed so that the limits and deductibles increase with inflation. The exposure hereunder is either third party bodily injury, third party property damage or else own physical damage from a windstorm or flood. Please note that the first two layers are silent on own damage losses, therefore they are covered! The main exposure hereunder is from bodily injury claims. Third party property damage claims and physical claims depend on the number of people involved, the types of injury and court awards.

This is not a class of business to underwrite unless you have a balanced portfolio, a good underwriter, a good computer system and an astute claims department. The main problem is that the awards do tend to increase greater than inflation and also there is no overall limit on most contracts. If there is a sudden award inflation we could end up with a large number of claims for 10 to 20 years.

Initial analysis

Pall Mall has a reasonable claims record. On looking at the triangulation of losses (p. 189) there are two major deteriorations. In 1989 where claim no. 6

has deteriorated to a current reserve of £950,000 and also claim no. 3 in 1986, which was settled for £750,000. Generally, they have had a few creeping losses and some which are reserved late.

We would need to have more details of the open claims to assess the claims management of the company. We would request to see the claims files of all outstanding losses over £100,000 reserve and ask if a meeting with the claims manager can be arranged. We would ask if we can have a historical record of the number of vehicles insured by year and any major changes in underwriting over the years.

The response was favourable: we looked at all open claim files and the reserves set seemed conservative. The major claim in 1988 was due to a gradual deterioration in condition of an injured person. The claim in 1986 was due to a case lost in the courts. The company indicated they would have settled the case earlier if the same situation arose.

The number of vehicles by year was received. The comment was that up until 1988 they used to insure taxis and buses but they discontinued due to adverse experience. From 1992 they decided to expand their account due to improvement in pricing and new sources of business. The most significant of these was a new direct telephone account biased towards lady drivers. This now represents 50% of their portfolio. The policy count is expected to stabilise in low-risk drivers and a stable book of non-standard business written at their head office. It is a well-spread book geographically with emphasis away from conurbations.

ASSESSMENT

1. On studying the policy count there has been a substantial growth over 10 years. Assuming the mix of business to be similar, the number of insured vehicles has increased by 1,000% since 1985. It is possible that the claims experience would have improved due to better claims management, lower-risk motorists and lower accident statistics. Unless any of the above can be substantiated the increase in policies means an increase in frequency.
2. The award inflation has been much worse than normal inflation in the last 10 years. Someone told me that peak awards had increased tenfold in 10 years; on applying a compound interest rate of 10% the inflation over 10 years would be 259%. This compound inflation rate seems too low to me. We will use an inflation rate of 15%. However, in view of the actual inflation of say 5%, which will affect the index, we will assume the inflation after the effect of the index is 15% − 5% = 10%.
3. The other problem with motor or long-tail claims is that they take a long time to develop and also some injuries develop late. Therefore,

there can be a deterioration in the size of the losses (severity) and an increase in the number of large claims (frequency). We need to produce an IBNR factor for these.
4. Using a computer we will multiply all reserves by a 10% compound interest factor to convert them to present day values, i.e. 1986—259%, 1987—235.8%, 1993—133.1%, etc.
5. We will also multiply all open claims by an IBNR factor to take care of future deterioration. This is judgemental:

> 1995 open claims 225%
> 1994 open claims 200%
> 1991 open claims 145%

These factors would depend on the reserving record of the company, etc. The work in 4 and 5 was done, but due to size is not shown here.
6. We have calculated the aggregated claims per year for each layer, i.e. £500,000 xs £500,000, etc. See Loss Cost table A p. 190. This would then be multiplied by the increase in policy count obtained from Pall Mall.
7. Finally we could multiply recent years by a further IBNR factor to account for claims not reserved above £100,000 yet. These calculations produce the figures in table C p. 191.
8. This method immediately exposes which layers are very underpriced: the first two. However, the third layer looks thin because one claim inflated breaches this layer. We will decline this, especially as this layer is exposed for physical damage losses. The top two layers are very high and the index clause at this level will help. The top layer is the best, although it is unlimited.
9. It is impossible for us as a follower to do the in-depth analysis needed, but our analysis shows us that the top two layers are the best priced. We have in this case considerable faith in the leader on this programme, in particular on the top two layers and in order to assist the broker we could write a modest line on these two layers. Therefore we could offer 7.5% on the top layer or 5% on the top two.
10. Please compare with Proposition 12a and 12b.

PROPOSITION 35

SLIP DETAILS

REASSURED: Syndicate No 3001 and for their quota share reinsurers.

PERIOD: Losses occurring during the period 12 months at 1 January 1995.

TYPE: EXCESS OF LOSS REINSURANCE.

CLASS: To indemnify the reassured in respect of all losses howsoever and wheresoever arising and designated by the reassured as aviation losses.

TERRITORIAL SCOPE: Losses wheresoever arising.

LIMITS: To pay up to: US/Can$500,000 excess of $50,000 each and every loss and/or occurrence and/or series of losses and/or occurrences arising out of one event.

WARRANTY: No loss to be recoverable hereunder unless there is a market loss of US$500,000,000 or greater.

REINSTATEMENTS: 1 full reinstatement at 100% additional premium.

PREMIUM: US$125,000 in full.

BROKERAGE: 10% (Nil on reinstatements).

GENERAL CONDITIONS: Ultimate net loss clause.
Common account reinsurance clause.
Market war, hijacking and allied perils clauses as included in original policies protected hereunder.
Extra contractual obligations clause (NMX 100).
Aviation grounding liability clause (1.12.81A) (1988 amendment).
Aviation grounding liability reinsurance clause.
Seepage and pollution exclusion clause SPEC II (1988 amendment).
Settlements clause 1987 (XL on XL).
Settlements clause 1987.
Non-renewal clause at terms to be agreed L/U only.
Excluding satellite losses.

AVIATION

1 Date	2 Airline/loss	3 War	4 Market loss US$ million	5 Est fatalities	6 1995 est loss US$ million
1977	Tenerife air crash		210	450?	1,000
1979	O'Hare airport crash		200	200?	600
1983	Korean air crash	war	175	250?	475
1985	Air India explosion	war	165	329	684
1985	Dallas air crash		200	136	390
1985	Japan air crash		445	520	850
1985	Newfoundland air crash		190	256	394
1987	Detroit air crash		290	156	440
1987	Mauritius air crash		105	159	368
1988	Lockerbie air crash	war	504	270	723
1990	Kuwait war	war	450	0	600
1991	Lauda Air		150	223	436
1992	La Guardia air crash		136	27	150

NB Six losses exceeding $500m.

COMMENTS

This is an unusual and a deceptive contract. Syndicate 3001's account is an aviation reinsurance account and should there be a market loss of $500,000,000 it will certainly have a loss of $550,000. Therefore, although the contract is phrased as an excess of loss, in effect it is a franchise and will pay a total loss of $500,000 each time there is a market loss as stipulated.

These franchise deals developed because of a lack of retrocessional capacity. There are a number of pitfalls in writing and buying these covers:

(a) If the market loss is one dollar less than the market loss specified, no loss is recoverable.
(b) Likewise if it is one dollar more, the full limit is recoverable.
(c) The market loss needs to be verified by some reliable body.

However, these are useful covers as they can be placed very quickly with the minimum of information. The reinsurers rely more on their own market loss data than on information.

Reinsurers and insurers need to be very careful how inflation of awards might affect market loss data.

ASSESSMENT

This is a market franchise for aviation losses; satellite losses are excluded but both physical damage and liability claims are included.

Good data has been provided by the broker showing market losses, fatalities and value of hull losses. Therefore, we can make some attempt to inflate these to present-day values. The main reason for large losses has been the large court awards to relatives of fatalities, largely in the USA. Awards of US$2,500,000 per person have been made. Awards on non-USA crashes are less but catching up.

I have assumed the awards would be US$2.5m per person for USA losses and US$1.5m for non-USA losses. For hull values I have assumed a doubling of values over 10 years. Figures shown in Column 6 of loss record (p. 195) are on this basis.

This calculation does not take into account the growth in air travel and the increase in passengers per aircraft.

This contract has a franchise of US$500m, therefore using my estimates there are six claims between 1977 and 1994 above US$500m. The terms of the contract are at a rate of 25%, i.e. (125,000/500,000) with one reinstatement at 100%.

As if 1977 to 1994:

premium received	17 × .25 = 4.25
reinstatement premium received	5 × .25 = 1.25
total premium	= 5.50
total claims	= 6.00

Therefore, the loss cost is greater than the premium, leaving no margin to cover brokerage, our own costs and profit margin. Therefore decline. If the price was increased to 30% rate then the total "as if" premium would be 6.9 units against claims of 6 units. With the potential investment income then we could perhaps consider a participation.

The body deciding the market loss or else the method of calculating it would have to be defined.

We obtained an exclusion of all war risks affecting more than one aircraft. Therefore the Kuwait loss and similar future exposures were excluded. We offered a $200,000 net line at a 25% rate on line with one reinstatement at 100%.

PROPOSITION 36

SLIP DETAILS

REINSURED: Lea Reinsurance Company.

PERIOD: Losses occurring during the 12 month period commencing from 1 January 1995 and ending with 31 December 1995 both days inclusive.

TYPE: EXCESS OF LOSS REINSURANCE.

CLASS: To indemnify the reinsured for all single risk losses of whatsoever nature in respect of all business underwritten by the reinsured.
Excluding:
(1) All business written specifically by the reinsured as liability business (other than as provided for in (5) below).
(2) Offshore marine (wording as attached).
(3) All aviation business including all launched satellite business (other than "pre-launch") *written specifically* as such.
(4) Life other than accidental death and dismemberment, Financial Guarantee and Insolvency.
(5) The reinsured's interest whether direct or by way of reinsurance in losses arising from claim or claims against an insured by another party or parties.
Notwithstanding the foregoing, this reinsurance shall not exclude:
  (i) Any Physical Damage and/or Consequential Loss coverage contingent thereon effected by an insured on behalf of another party.
  (ii) Any incidental liability losses arising out of Homeowners' policies/Commercial fire policies and the like (or sections of policies).
  (iii) Any incidental Property Damage Liability losses arising out of Owners' or Tenants' Liability.
(6) Transmission and Distribution Lines, wording as expiring.
(7) Losses arising under policies *specifically* written by the reinsured as catastrophe reinsurance irrespective of whether these policies are written

to London Market or overseas insureds or reinsureds, *other than* in respect of single risk losses arising thereunder, which shall be expressly protected hereunder.

(8) Liability arising out of any excess of loss and/or pro-rata reinsurances incepting on or after 1 January 1993 issued in the name of and for the account of a Lloyd's syndicate or of an insurance or reinsurance company, whether such liability is accepted either directly or under any form of reinsurance from other insurers and/or reinsurers, and all such liability is excluded from the protection of this reinsurance and cannot be taken into account in arriving at the amount in excess of which this reinsurance attaches. The reinsured shall be the sole judge as to which insurance or reinsurance companies come within the scope of this definition.

Notwithstanding the foregoing, it is understood and agreed that:

Excess of loss and/or pro-rata reinsurances of direct and facultative accounts shall not fall within the scope of the above definition.

TERRITORIAL SCOPE: Losses wheresoever occurring.

LIMIT: To pay up to: £500,000 or US$750,000 each and every original risk.

Event Limit: Subject to a maximum recoverable of £500,000 or US$/CAN$750,000 arising from any one event.

In excess of an ultimate net loss of: £500,000 or US$/CAN$750,000 each and every original risk.

REINSTATEMENT: Two full reinstatements each calculated at pro rata (as to indemnity only) of 100% additional premium.

PREMIUM: Adjustable at 1.60% of the reinsured's applicable net premium income "accounted for" during 12 months at 1 January 1995.

On Risk excess business, plus 0.60% of the reinsured's applicable net premium income "accounted for" in respect of their pro rata account during the period 12 months at 1 January 1995.

Minimum and Deposit Premium: £120,000 plus US$120,000 payable in four equal instalments on 1 January, 1 April, 1 July and 1 October 1995.

DEDUCTIONS:	10% brokerage (nil on reinstatement).
CONDITIONS:	Ultimate net loss clause, amended to allow the reinsured to have the benefit of recoveries on underlying excess of loss reinsurances, if any.

Reinsured to be the sole judge as to what constitutes "each and every original risk".

All terms, clauses, conditions and warranties as original and to follow original settlements in every respect, so far as applicable.

London Market extra contractual obligations clause (NMX100) (additional premium included in premium).

Standard run-off clause No. 3 risks written basis.

All losses to be considered in chronological loss date order.

Extended expiration clause.

Definition of any one event.

Currency clause (amended for losses wholly or partially payable in US and/or Canadian dollars, where a rate of exchange of US$/CAN$1.50 = £1.00 will apply).

Notification of loss clause.

Errors and omissions clause (as expiring).

Inspection of records clause (as expiring).

Amendments and alterations clause.

Arbitration clause as expiring (law of England to be the proper law of this reinsurance).

War and civil war exclusion clause G51 (UK amendment), wording as expiring.

Insolvency cancellation clause as expiring.

Nuclear energy risks exclusion clause reinsurance (1984) NMA 1975 (Japanese amendment) and Nuclear incident exclusion clauses reinsurance United States of America/Canada.

2nd Layer $1,500,000 × 1,500,000 1 reinstatement pro rata for amount 100% for time.
Rates 2.0% on Risk excess plus 0.75% on pro rata minimum and deposit £150,000 US$150,000.

INFORMATION:

Estimated accounted premiums in millions

	Risk Excess			Pro Rata		
	£	US$	Total in US$	£	US$	Total in US$
1993	4.0	2.8	8.8	2.3	1.25	4.7
1994	6.0	3.5	12.50	3.4	1.1	6.2
1995 (est)	8.0	4.0	16	3.6	1.0	6.4

Underwriting limits

		Absolute Max
International Risk XL	– Programme	£1,250,000
USA Risk XL	– Programme	US$1,750,000
London Market Risk Excess	– Programme	US$1,000,000
International Pro Rata	– Programme	US$750,000
USA Pro Rata	– Programme	US$1,750,000

Losses

Loss exceeding £200,000 or US$300,000 fgu:

DOL	Original Insured	No of Contracts	No of Progs	US$ Incurred
23.10.89	Phillips Petroleum		7	520,000
26.02.93	WTC		6	450,000
04.10.93	Xetex Korea		4	460,000
14.11.93	Texas Utilities		15	750,000
06.04.94	Wierton Steel		1	640,000

COMMENTS

This is a retrocessional property risk programme. Risk profiles and rate on line profiles (not produced here for space reasons) showed the company's lines to be mainly on middle or upper layers with normal exposures per programme below US$500,000 and £250,000.

The company has grown quickly but now levelling off.
The account is predominantly outside the USA.
The record is good.

ASSESSMENT

In order to discover cost of past losses as if they occurred in 1995 we used two computer projections. One on the basis of premium increase and second the increase in line limits (not shown here). These produced some odd results, e.g. the Phillips loss became $6m on premium income basis but only $1.6m on line increase. We thought that an "as if" figure of $3,000,000 was sensible. Our "as if" losses from ground up became:

1989	Phillips	$3,000,000
1993	WTC	800,000
1993	Xetex	850,000
1993	Texas Utilities	1,130,000
1994	Wierton Steel	650,000

This gave us an "as if" loss experience on the two layers as follows:

		1st layer 750,000 × 750,000	2nd layer 1,500,000 × 1,500,000
1989	Phillips	750,000	1,500,000
1993	WTC	50,000	
1993	Texas Utilities	380,000	NIL
1993	Xetex	100,000	
		1,280,000	1,500,000
6 years burn		$213,000	$250,000

Premium offered

First layer: $300,000
Second layer: $375,000

The first layer is a "money swap" with a ROL of 40% but a fair one. The second layer with little or no exposure per programme and only one reinstatement looks attractive for two reasons. Phillips may be overstated and a good deal of 1995 exposures will be on 1994 or even 1993 lines.

Write 10% net on second excess and perhaps 2½% on the first excess.

A UTOPIAN POSTCRIPT
1996–2010

The Company flourished in 1996–1998 in a competitive market and by the end of 1998 had spread worldwide and established good reinsurance accounts in eastern Europe and the East. It scaled down some of its commitments in the USA, the Americas and Japan, which enabled it to survive better than some, the cataclysmic earthquakes and storms that heralded the end of the old millenium and the start of the new.

The general deterioration in results in Europe due to the failure of continental protectionist economies and the ensuing unrest and riots did not greatly affect us.

The expulsion of Britain from the European Federation by the Edict of Dunkirk in AD 2001 (the "Great Release") caused a run on the pound sterling and inflation. This led to the introduction in 2002 AD of the Albion pound equal to 10 pounds sterling. This caused a drastic increase in UK Motor and Third Party claims so that £5,000,000 (old sterling) per person was a commonplace award. Once that was over, the recovery of London's position as the financial and insurance centre of the world was dramatic. This was due in no small measure to the liberal tax treatment (with income tax at 10%) introduced by the new government of the sovereign "Islands of Albion" (England, Wales, Scotland, Ireland, Ulster, Channel Islands, Isle of Man, Fair Isle and Iceland). In particular the tax free status for policy holders' reserves greatly strengthened our position *vis-à-vis* the Federation of Europe (FOE), the USA and Bermuda.

By 2010 AD the Utopian was a reinsurance force worldwide with a capital and surplus of Albion £300,000,000 (US $1,500,000,000) on a revived London Market.

Stephen Kiln retired honourably at the end of 2009 AD with a pension of old sterling of £1,500,000 per annum. His father Robert, having been on a course of hormones, steroids, whisky and having had a brain transplant, returned to take over again in 2010 AD aged 92.

Per ardua ad astra.

INDEX

Accident treaties
   assessment and, 77
   example of, 76–78
   first surplus treaty and, 76–78
   information and, 77
Accounts, 23, 24
   cash-flow control and, 35
   long-tail, 33
Accumulation exposures, 20–22
   aviation liabilities and, 22
   cargo excesses and, 22
   excess of loss reinsurance and, 20–22
   exposure control and, 20–22
   latent exposures and, 22
   marine hull excesses and, 22
   professional indemnity claims and, 22
   reinsurance protection and, 21–22
   retrocession and, 20
   third party excesses and, 22
Aggregation extension clauses, 18
Analysis codes, 118
Asbestos liabilities, 31–32
Assessment
   accident treaties and, 77
   aviation excess of loss and, 107
   casualty excess of loss and, 97–99, 104
   excess loss catastrophe and, 67–69, 157–158, 161, 170–172, 176–177
   excess of loss and, 78–79, 123, 148–149, 152–154, 192–193, 196, 200–201
      first per risk, 71–73, 92
      second layer, 86, 114–115
      third layer, 86–87
   fire treaties and, 50, 54–55, 67–69
   first obligatory surplus and, 47
   German motor damage excess of loss and, 88–89
   marine excess of loss and, 107, 112
   medical treaties and, 132
   obligatory quota share treaty and, 184–185
   quota share treaty and, 58–59, 61–62
   retrocession and, 82–83
   stop loss treaties and, 75
   surplus treaties and, 127–128

Aviation hull treaties
   examples of, 105–107
   excess of loss and, 105–107
   exposure controls and, 22
   line limits and, 5
   losses, 196
   maximum net lines and, 8

Board of directors, 3

Capital, 2, 4–8
Cargo treaties
   exposure controls and, 22
   line limits and, 5
   reinsurance protection and, 18–19
Cash-flow control, 35
   accounts and, 35
   commissions and, 35
   deposit premiums and, 35
   excess business and, 35
   interest and, 35
   reserves and, 35
Casualty excess of loss
   assessment and, 97–99, 104
   examples of, 93–104
   information and, 96–97, 103
Catastrophe. *See* Excess loss catastrophe contracts
Commission, 17, 35
Computers, 28–29, 118
Currency, 34–35
   fluctuation clauses, 64
   reserves and, 33, 34

Data, 23
Decision-taking, 35–36
Deposit premiums, 35
Directors, 3
Discounting
   interest and, 34
   reserves and, 34
   run-offs and, 34
Disputes, 39–40

Earthquakes, 135, 137–138, 163, 170–171, 176
Estimates, 23–24
　loss ratio and, 33
　reserves and, 33
Examples
　accident treaty and, 76–78
　aviation excess of loss, 105–107
　casualty excess of loss, 93–104
　excess loss catastrophe, 63–69, 133–145, 155–162, 166–180
　excess of loss, 63–73, 78–79, 84–107, 113–115, 119–125, 146–154, 187–200
　fire treaties, 49–56
　German motor damage excess of loss, 88–89
　marine excess of loss, 105–107
　medical treaties, 130–132
　obligatory first surplus, 45–48
　obligatory quota share treaty, 181–186
　quota share treaty, 56–62
　retrocession, 80–83
　second surplus, 108–110
　special hull first surplus treaty, 111–112
　stop loss, 74–75
　surplus, 126–129
Excess aggregate reinsurance
　line limits and, 7
　maximum net lines and, 9
Excess loss catastrophe contracts
　aides-memoires and, 42
　assessment and, 67–69, 136–140, 144–145, 157–158, 161, 170–172, 176–177
　currency fluctuation clause and, 64
　examples of, 63–69, 133–145, 155–162, 166–180
　first layer, 159–162
　information and, 66, 134–136, 143–144, 156–157, 160–161
　　first layer, 175, 179–180
　　third layer, 167–170
　line limits and, 5
　loss occurrences and, 64–66
　market, 164
　maximum net lines and, 8, 17
　outwards protection, 24
　protection, 17–18
Excess loss treaties. *See also* Excess loss catastrophe contracts
　aides-memoire and, 43
　assessment and, 192–193, 196, 200–201
　aviation, 105–106
　cash-flow control and, 35
　casualty, 93–104
　currency fluctuation clause and, 64
　examples of, 63–73, 78–79, 84–107, 113–115, 119–125, 146–154, 187–201
　expenses and, 11, 13–14
　first per risk, 70–73

Excess loss treaties—*cont.*
　German motor damage, 88–89
　information and, 78, 121–123, 147–148, 151–152, 200–201
　　aviation, 106–107
　　casualty, 96–97, 103
　　first layer, 90–92
　　first per risk, 70–71
　　marine, 106–107
　　second layer, 114
　　third layer, 86
　layers, 6
　loss occurrences and, 64–66
　marine, 105–107
　recording liabilities and, 24–25
　reinsurance protection and, 20
　second surplus, 108–110
Expenses, 11–15
　claims, 23–24
　excess loss and, 11, 13–14
　facultative reinsurances and, 11, 13
　maximum ratios for, 11
　pro rata treaties and, 11–13
　profits and, 11
　stop loss reinsurance and, 11, 13–14
Exposure controls, 20–22
　aviation liabilities and, 22
　cargo excesses and, 22
　marine hull excesses and, 22
　professional indemnity claims and, 22
　reinsurance protection and, 21, 22
　third party and, 22
Exposure limits, 4

Facultative R/Is
　aides-memoire and, 44
　expenses and, 11, 13
　line limits and, 8
　outwards, 24
Fire treaties, 49–55
　assessment and, 50–51, 54–55, 67–69
　currency fluctuation clause and, 64
　examples of, 49–51, 63–69
　information and, 50, 52–53, 54, 66
　loss occurrences and, 64–66
Floods, 138–140
Foreign exchange, 1

German motor damage excess of loss, 88–89
Government reinsurance operation, 1

Hail treaties, 138–140
　line limits and, 5
　maximum net lines and, 8
　reinsurance protection and, 19
Hurricanes, 138–140, 163–165, 169

Incurred but not reported reserves, 25, 31, 33
Inflation, 33, 34

Index

Information, 23
  accident treaties and, 77
  analysis codes and, 118
  catastrophe excess loss and, 66–68, 134–136, 143–144, 156–157, 160–161, 179–180
  excess of loss and, 78, 121–123, 147–148, 151–152, 167–170, 175, 200–201
    aviation, 106–107
    casualty, 96–97, 103
    first layer, 90–92
    first per risk, 70–71
    marine, 106–107
    second layer, 114
    third layer, 86
  fire treaties and, 50, 54
  German motor damage excess of loss and, 88–89
  obligatory first surplus and, 46–47
  quota share treaties and, 57, 61, 81–82
  retrocessions and, 81–82, 164
  stop loss and, 74–75
  surplus treaties and, 127
  underwriting examples and, 41–115, 119–161
Interest
  cash-flow control and, 35
  discounting and, 34
  reserves and, 34
Investment
  funds of, 4
  premium fund of, 35
  reserves and, 35

Line limits, 4–8
  capital and, 4
  cargo treaties and, 5
  excess aggregate reinsurances and, 7
  excess loss catastrophe contracts and, 5–6
  excess of layers and, 6
  facultative R/Is and, 8
  hail treaties and, 5
  livestock treaties and, 5
  marine and aviation hull treaties and, 5
  maximum net lines and, 8–9
  motor excess contracts and, 7
  personal accident treaties and, 5
  pro rata property treaties and, 4
  stop loss reinsurances and, 7
  third party liability and, 7
  war treaties and, 5
Livestock treaties, 5, 8
Lloyd's syndicates, 2
Long-tail business
  accounts and, 33
  estimated loss ratio and, 33
  profit and, 3–4
  reserves and, 31, 32, 33–34

Loss occurrences
  definition of, 64–66
  excess loss catastrophe and, 64–66
  excess of loss treaties and, 64–66
  fire treaties and, 64–66

Management team, 3–4
  decision-making and, 35–37
  integrity and, 37–38
Marine hull treaties
  assessment and, 107, 112
  examples of, 105–107, 111–112
  excess of loss and, 105–107
  exposure controls and, 22
  information and, 106–107
  line limits and, 5
  maximum net lines and, 8
  reinsurance protection and, 18–19
  special hull first surplus treaty and, 111–112
Maximum net lines, 8–9
  excess loss catastrophe contracts and, 17
  outwards treaty programme and, 14
Maximum percentage lines, 9
Medical treaties
  assessment and, 132
  examples of, 130–132
Medium-tail business, 31, 33
Motor excess contracts, 191–193
  aides-memoire and, 43
  example of, 88–89
  German, 88–89
  line limits and, 7

Obligatory first surplus
  assessment of, 47, 184–185
  example of, 45–48, 181–186
  information and, 46–47
Oil rigs, 18–19, 184–186
Outwards facultative reinsurance, 24

Personal accident treaties
  line limits and, 5
  maximum net lines and, 8
Political risks, 19
Pollution liabilities, 31–32
Premium fund investment, 35
Pro rata property treaties, 4, 11
Probable Maximum Loss, 4
Professional indemnity claims, 22
Profit, 3–4
  investment, 11
  long-tail business and, 3–4
  underwriting, 11
Property treaties
  line limits and, 8
  market, 163
  maximum net lines and, 8
  pro rata, 4

Protection
  accumulation exposures and, 17, 20
  aggregate extension clauses and, 18
  cargo insurance and, 18–19
  catastrophe, 17–18
  exposure controls and, 21, 22
  hail business and, 19
  marine hull insurance and, 18–19
  maximum net lines and, 17
  oil rig insurance and, 18–19
  political risks and, 19
  retrocession and, 20
  stop loss reinsurance and, 19
  third party reinsurance and, 18
  war risks and, 19

Quota share treaty, 56–62
  assessment and, 58–59, 61–62
  examples of, 59–62, 80–83
  information and, 57, 61
  retrocession and, 80–83

Records, 23, 24–25
Reserves, 31–34
  accounts and, 33
  asbestos liabilities and, 31–32
  assumed loss ratio and, 31, 33
  cash-flow control and, 35
  currency and, 33, 34
  discounting and, 34
  incurred but not reported, 25, 31, 33
  inflation and, 33
  interest and, 34
  investment and, 35
  Lloyd's and, 34
  long-tail business and, 31, 32, 33–34
  medium-tail business and, 31, 33
  pollution liabilities and, 31–32
  results and, 31
  run-offs and, 34
  settlement percentage and, 32
  short-tail business and, 31, 33
  statistics and, 31
Retrocession, 17
  accumulation exposures and, 20
  assessments and, 82–83
  example of, 80–83
  hurricanes and, 164
  information and, 81–82, 164
  quota share, 80–83
  spiral markets and, 163
Risks
  acceptance of, 3
  aides-memoire and, 43
  excess contracts, 8, 43
Run-offs
  discounting and, 34
  reserves and, 34

Settlement, 32
Short-tail business, 31, 33
Slips, examples of, 41–115, 119–161
Statistics, 24, 25–28, 31, 109, 118
Stop loss reinsurance
  aides-memoire and, 43–44
  assessment and, 75
  example of, 74–75
  expenses and, 11, 13–14
  inwards business, 24–25
  information and, 74–75
  line limits and, 7
  recording liabilities and, 24–25
  reinsurance protection and, 19
Surplus treaties, 14
  accident, 76–78
  assessment and, 127–128
  examples of, 45–48, 76–78, 108–112, 126–129
  first obligatory, 45–48
  information and, 127
  second surplus, 108–110
  special hull first, 111–112
Systems and controls, 23–29
  accounts and, 23
  analyis codes and, 118
  claims and, 23–24
  computers and, 28–29
  estimates and, 24
  excess of loss business and, 24–25
  excess of loss outwards protection and, 24
  expenses and, 23
  incurred but not reported reserves and, 25
  information and, 23
  outwards facultative reinsurance and, 24
  outwards reinsurances and, 24
  records and, 23–24
  statistics and, 24, 25–28
  stop loss inwards business and, 24
  underwriting data and, 23

Third party liability contracts
  aides-memoire and, 43
  exposure controls and, 22
  line limits and, 7
  maximum percentage lines and, 9
  reinsurance protection and, 18
Tornados, 138
Treaties. *See also* Particular treaties
  aides-memoire and, 42
  outwards treaty programme and, 14–15, 24
  quota share, 14
  surplus, 14
Typhoons, 180

Underwriting
  aides-memoire and, 42–44
  constructive, 39–40
  disputes and, 39–40

Underwriting—*cont.*
   examples, 41–115

War treaties
   line limits and, 5

War treaties—*cont.*
   maximum net lines and, 8

Windstorms, 163, 171–172

Workmen's compensation, 43